THE LASH

BY NICHOLAS CASEY

Nothing matters more than the game

www.thelash.eu

wolfridge

Warning: Play games at your own risk

Please be aware that alcohol is a drug and I would class it as one of the most ruinous and expensive addictions around. Alcohol abuse is a contributing factor to many diseases and being intoxicated can lead to injury or even death. A games inclusion is not a recommendation to its implementation. Carefully consider what you drink.

Enough of the lecture! After you've read and understood my little disclaimer below, we'll never talk about such serious things again!

A word from my lawyer: "The games contained in this book are undertaken at the reader's own risk. The author, Nicholas Johnathon Casey, accepts no liability whatsoever for the way in which the reader uses the information contained in this book. It is the reader's responsibility to ensure that only adults above the legal age for purchasing alcohol participant in the games and that the games are conducted in a responsible manner."

Written and project managed by Nicholas Johnathon Casey (nicholaskc@googlemail.com)

Design by Abi Renshaw (abi_renshaw@hotmail.co.uk)

Proof reading & editorial work by Abi Renshaw, Caroline Low & Taissa Csaky (virgoeditorial@email.com)

Web design for *www.wolfridgepublishing.co.uk* by Chris Davis @ iTechGenie (chris@itechgenie.co.uk)

Web design for *www.thelash.eu* by Nicholas Skehin (nicholas.skehin@gmail.com)

All illustration Copyright © Lucy Joy Oldfield (*www.lucyjoyoldfield.com*)

All photography Copyright © Joanna Webster (*www.joannawebsterphotography.co.uk*)

Produced in 2008 by Wolfridge Limited
(for information on this title see *www.thelash.eu*)

Published and printed in 2008 by Lightning Source UK Ltd.
Chapter House, Pitfield, Kiln Farm, Milton Keynes MK11 3LW
Email: enquiries@lightningsource.co.uk
Voice: 0845 121 4567
Fax: 0845 121 4594
www.lightningsource.com

ISBN: 978-0-9558644-0-7

Printed in Great Britain

wolfridge

loving, living, learning.
in progress.

life Student·tv

In association with *www.lifeisastudent.com*

This book is dedicated to Abi Renshaw:
Abi took on this project when all I had was rambling notes. She gave structure and organisation to madness! At all times, she has been my point of reference for everything technical, providing consultation well outside of her 'design for print' remit. Without her support and guidance there would be no book. I owe a vast debt to you Abi, for realising my dreams for *The Lash*!

Thanks must go to my parents for having to answer the question "What's Nick doing?" They never once showed anything but 100% confidence in me.

Thanks also go to my many friends who gave up their time for free during filming and photo shoots. A massive thank you goes to those who used their skills to aid this project: most notably Abi, Lucy, Jo, Chris D, Martin, Nick and Chrissy. Many thanks to Caroline and Taissa who took on the project at such short notice. Thanks also goes out to Kieran who kept an old dog current on the lash, plus Matt and Dave who never stopped hearing about 'the book!' Big thanks also goes out to Sarah, Mikey, Nathan and Christine who all gave up their free time to read through *The Lash* one last time. And finally, a very special thanks goes to Mrs Gale who worked so hard and asked for nothing.

Contents

🔥	easy
🔥	medium
🔥	hard
🔥	extreme

Introduction

So what is *The Lash* all about?
A drinking game will not spontaneously operate. For it to succeed, there must be an Administrator who explains the games to all and is the authority who prevents anarchy from reining. *The Lash* is there to teach you how to play 35 very different drinking games suited to a variety of occasions. Once you have learnt the games, you can go on to educate others when you next get a lash on.

The language
All the games contained within *The Lash* are as I have learnt them and the way in which my friends and I play them. The language is British university lash, raw and un-doctored. Like any language there are many dialects so translate them into your own banter so the games take on your own style and quirks. Please do not get put off as all words are referenced to the glossary where they are explained.

Glossary references
All words, which I consider need explanation, are bold e.g. **lash**. You will find lash in the glossary under L. If there is more than one word in bold, I have put the letter which is relevant for searching in brackets after the word e.g. **hard lash (L)** or **mad drunk (M)**.

If the same word has multiple meanings e.g. **call**, I have numbered all the relevant meanings of that word under its reference in the glossary. Therefore, refer to the number after the word to look up its meaning, i.e. **call**[4].

Make the game suit you
Once you know a game inside out, you can make it suit you in a number of ways. You can incorporate your own quirks and style, so the game suits the people playing and the environment in which you are playing. You may have played several drinking games in *The Lash* but under different names. You may also find that the game I describe is a variation of a game you already know. This is great! There is no right and wrong way to play these games. Variations are inherent in drinking games. Drinking games have no stead fast rules as they are like chameleons,

forever changing because of their social origins. *The Lash* is simply a point of reference to remind you of some **legendary** games. Always do what is most fun for you and add you own style to the games. You will find no generic games here, as the social context is what gives these games life. This book aims to introduce you to drinking games you haven't met before and suggest new ways to play the games you may already know. *The Lash* is simply a selection of great drinking games, which have been tried and tested.

My philosophy regarding the Administrator

In every game there must be a **Boss** or **Administrator**. This is the person who is in social control of the situation and dishes out the fines. They are the **the law (L)**. I believe in ruling drinking games with an **iron fist (I)** and this is why the book is subtitled 'Nothing matters more than the game.' If you're in charge, you'll need to be harsh to keep the game flowing. You can't let anything get in the way of the game or you'll find it will fall apart, as focus is important. Drinking games teach manners, self confidence and co-ordination and are designed to be inclusive. The very fact that a drinking game passes around allows everyone to be involved.

The layout of the book

It is often the case that one drinking game has been spawned from another. An 'original' (I use this very loosely for there is no such thing in terms of drinking games) is followed by its relations. For example, 'Pyramid Cheat' comes after 'Pyramid'.

Please don't be put off by long explanations, as some of the most rewarding games take some explaining. Drinking games by their very nature are confusing. But fear not, you'll notice that they are also logical, so it only takes one moment of clarity to gain an understanding.

The layout of each game

Under each game, I have given a brief description, explained the number of players needed, the ideal situation, the drinks needed, the difficulty of the game, the intoxication level, the implements needed, the games' shelf life and a more detailed explanation, all in order for you to decide quickly if this is the game for you and your friends to play. Pull the wrong game out at the wrong moment and even the best game will fail to impress.

Brief description
This gives you an idea of the basics. You may be able to start playing by using only this description. These are guiding notes at a glance.

Number of players
This indicates the ideal number of players for the game. Here you will also find the minimum to maximum number of players needed.

Situation
It is very important that you understand that every drinking game has a time and a place. Deciding when to play a certain drinking game is a subtle art. You must be able to gage what sort of 'time' everyone is having and also take into account the make up of the group. If it's just a social drink then initiating some **hard lash (L)** is not going to work. If there are some people present who take themselves quite seriously then asking players to pull animal faces (see 'Animal Kingdom' on p130) isn't going to make you any friends. You must think before you implement a game. From my experience, I will guide you on what sorts of conditions are best for a games' success. In practice you are forced to make your own judgement on which game will best suit the moment you find yourself.

Drinks needed
Often specific types of drink are needed. Check what everyone is drinking before picking a game. Can everyone afford to buy the drinks needed in the volumes required?

Difficulty
The grades of difficulty are:
- Easy
- Medium
- Hard
- Complex

Difficulty is a combination of how hard it is to understand and how challenging it is to play.

Intoxication level
The grades for intoxication are:
- Low (a social drink)
- Medium
- High
- Extreme (carnage!)

Implements needed
Some games will need specific implements. These are usually different types and sizes of drinking vessels, cards or coins. Sometimes specific furniture is required, or on rare occasions, other oddities specific to the game may be needed. I have tried to pick games that don't need much more than you, your mates and some drinks.

Shelf life
Every game has a shelf life, i.e. how long it takes for the game to become monotonous. You must be able to recognise this and make a smooth transition to another game. Every game will get boring, although some attain this state of boredom more quickly than others. Therefore I've given them a one to five star rating to indicate their shelf life.

The grading for shelf life:
☆ One star (will probably only last a **round**[2])
☆☆☆☆☆ Five stars (keep you entertained for most of your adult life)

The game in more detail
This is the full explanation of the game and often contains diagrams, examples, pictures and in some circumstances, an Info+. This gives handy information and tips aside from the explanation in order to make the game run more smoothly and improve your game play!

Now let the games begin!

Chapter 1
Straight Lash Games

 ## Case Race

Brief description
Two teams race to be the first to finish their case of **beer**!

Number of players
It's best to have four or more players on each team. More players per team will make the game **softer**. Less players per team will do the opposite and make the game **savage**! If you play with only two players per team, I'd say you've got a **head tap (H)** and you'll need to phone and tell the hospital to prepare the stomach pump!

Situation
BBQ or **pre-lash (P)**. This game is **messy**, so it's best to be outdoors or in a room that can handle a few spillages.

Drinks needed
Two cases of beer (also see **slab**). In England the case unit is twenty-four cans. However this game can also be played with bottles or smaller boxes to make it easier.

Difficulty
Easy

Intoxication level
Extreme

Implements needed
Two cases of beer. See above.

Shelf life ☆☆
You'll play this again but not on the same day as it's not the subtlest of games.

The game explained in detail

This game needs very little explanation. Teams go head-to-head in a race to be first to finish their case. Teamwork is encouraged. With four players per team this means six cans each. If anyone goes **man-down (M)** then other team members must either provide encouragement or **step up (S)** to help their ailing team mate finish.

The team that comes last, will not only earn the scorn of their peers, but in some cases could be fined. I suggest a good fine for losing is an extra can of drink per player, which has to be **chinned**. This will not be popular after consuming so much gassy beer and makes for a frantic competition during the race. In this 'case' the players in the team which comes second really are the first losers!

Centurion

Brief description

This is the easiest explanation in *The Lash*. The idea is to drink one hundred shots of beer in 100 minutes. I know **brainiac** that's a shot a minute for 100 minutes! Sounds easy? Give it a go!

Number of players

Two players or more but please don't play on your own!

Situation

The ultimate **pre-lash (P)** game.

Drinks needed

Beer or cider in large quantities. A large can of Stella is around 500ml. You'll need approximately five cans to finish. The big two litre 'tramp' cider bottles can be useful for this game.

Tramp cider — perfect for when you need vast volumes of cheap booze

Difficulty
Easy
INFO+ Easier than getting a gun in the US!

Intoxication level
High

Implements needed
A 25ml shot glass per player and a watch or clock.

Shelf life ☆☆☆
You'll play this game again but not back-to-back on the same day.

Next!

Brief description
Chin your drink and pass the **go** on by tapping your glass against the glass of the next player (see **E.T.**).

Number of players
Three players or more.

Situation
A loud night **out²** on a **Hard lash (L)**.

Drinks needed
Any

Difficulty
Easy
INFO+ The easiest game to learn but a hard game to play. This will hurt!

Intoxication level
Extreme

Implements needed
Nothing other than alcoholic liquid in some sort of drinking vessel.

Shelf life ☆☆☆
So long as like-minded individuals are present, this game makes an appearance at least once on every night out². It now constitutes a **game of life (G)** for me. It's a great way to start a chain reaction of chaos to marvel at once you have finished your drink!

The game explained in detail
A game of 'Next!' can be started by anyone, although you must have the personal authority to make sure that it will be continued or you'll look rather silly. Start the game off by **downing** your drink. If there is quite a

volume of liquid, this may draw the attention of those around you. Then say "Next!" and tap the glass of the player nearest to you. The player whose glass has been tapped then downs their drink and similarly passes the go on with a tap. Once the go returns to the player who started the game, if they have another drink in, they can send the go round again. Usually though, one **round²** of 'Next!' will suffice. This game might sound rather stupid but it definitely strengthens group dynamics and ensures everyone starts a new **round¹** of drinks at the same time.

Boat Race

Brief description
Quickest team to drink all their drinks one after another wins the boat race. This game is known as 'boat race' because you are lined up like the crew of a rowing boat and must work as a team. It is usually played 8 vs 8 like the teams in the **Varsity** Boat Race.

Number of players
This game is played in teams. More than four players in a team is a prerequisite for a good game. However, numbers in each team must be equal. I believe that the game improves as the numbers of players per team increases.

Situation
A rowdy bar or a sports club bar, or even a **lash** BBQ.

Drinks needed
A full pint per player.

Difficulty
Easy
INFO+ Easy to learn but it is a skill to **chin** a pint at speed whilst under pressure.

Intoxication level
Medium
INFO+ Depends on how many **rounds**[2] you play.

Implements needed
Friends and plenty of pints.

Shelf life ☆☆☆
This game is entertaining so long as there is competition.

The game in more detail

Get into two teams or, if in a sporting environment, challenge your competitors in the bar after the game. Line up one after another in **Indian file (I)** like you're a rowing team.

Each player has a full pint. The players are counted into the race by a neutral observer, who says "go!". On the one, two, three 'go' Player 1 of each team drinks their pint as fast as they can. When they have finished their pint they put the glass upside down on top of their head and hold it there.

Players 1 and 2 have downed their pints and Player 3 has started on his

This is a signal for Player 2, standing next in line, to start drinking. You can only start drinking if the person in front has finished their pint and turned their glass up on their head to prove it. Going before the person in front of you has finished is massively **frowned upon (F)** because it is cheating.

The whole line or 'boat' can get held up by one slow drinker. Likewise a faster drinker can **pull it back (P)** for your team. One tactic is to put your fastest drinker on what is **called[7]** the **anchor leg (A)**, i.e. the last place in the line.

The winning team is the first to have all players holding empty pint glasses on their heads. The losing team must buy the winning team a fresh round of drinks.

You could hold a rematch if the race was particularly close, or if one of the teams isn't satisfied with their performance or the result, however the winning team has the final say on this.

As soon as the player in front has turned their glass over, the next player starts to drink

Panic Button

Brief description

Drink as much or as little as you like when a vessel containing alcoholic drink is passed to you. However be warned! If the player who has their go after you successfully **downs** the remaining liquid in the vessel **in one (O)** the consequence for you will be a fine. The fine in 'Panic Button' is always to drink the entirety of a refilled vessel!

Number of players

You want at least four players or more to play this game, though in theory you could play with two players. A two player game would result in you and your friend both **downing** a considerable volume of drink. The more players, the more the burden is shared. I like a game to have at least six players.

Situation

In an understanding bar or pub. If you don't have one of these nearby, then use a private residence (i.e. someone's house). This is **pre-lash (P)** on a grand scale.

Drinks needed

You are going to fill a vessel with at least two and half pints which will be drunk twice over each **round**[2] so something not too strong. **Beer**, cider or watered down **spirits** with flat coke or lemonade (bubbles make downing much harder) are perfect.

Difficulty

Easy

INFO+ The concept is not difficult but the downing can be if you panic.

Intoxication level

Extreme

INFO+ This game is **savage!** Although it will not last many **rounds**[2] there is a possibility of drinking huge volumes of drink in one. Proceed with caution — this is not for the **faint-hearted (F)**!

Implements needed

A **yard glass (Y)** (this holds 2.5 pints), a **Stein**, a drinking boot **called**[7] a **Stiefel** or simply a jug that holds lots of drink. Certain drinking establishments have vessels such as these behind the bar.

Shelf life ☆☆☆

Entertaining, but unless you're looking to get **cirrhosis of the liver (C)** you won't play this more than once on a particular night!

The game in more detail

A large quantity of drink (at least 2.5 pints) in the Stein/yard/Stiefel/ jug ('the Vessel') is passed around a circle either to the left or right. The direction does not change once the game has started. On your **go** you can drink as much or as little liquid as you want from the Vessel. However the rule is that if the player after you finishes the drink (and this must be in one attempt, i.e. **chinning** it) then you have to drink *all* of a refilled vessel as a fine. The player fined must *drink the refilled vessel quickly*, as everyone has to wait for them to finish before restarting the game, but they do *not* have to drink it down in one. To restart the game, the Vessel is refilled for a third time and starts with the player who has just been fined taking the first drink.

This game's full title is 'Press the Panic Button' because when players start to worry that the person after them will drain the Vessel, they panic and down what's left themselves, to ensure they do not have to drink a refilled vessel.

INFO+ Be aware of the critical mass level of the Vessel. This is a point where players will fancy that they can finish the liquid content of the Vessel **in one** attempt. At the critical mass level downing what remains is less of a fine than drinking the whole vessel refilled. Different players will have different critical mass levels depending on their drinking ability.

Tip

Try not to stand before a **lash monster (L)**. The fine for this game is obviously horrendous. But if you want to make the **lash** even more savage, mix the games 'Panic Button' and 'The Challenge' (p16) together.

The Challenge

Brief description
A jug is passed round and players contribute part of their drink to it. The jug is now **called**[7] the Challenge and is redistributed for consumption.

Number of players
More than two players.

Situation
Moderate to **hard lash (L)**. Any establishment which accepts the mixing of drinks.

Drinks needed
Any but preferably lots of different ones.

Difficulty
Easy

Intoxication level
High
INFO+ Especially when **spirits** are involved.

Implements needed
A jug and plenty of half pint glasses. A pack of cards for Option 2 below.

Shelf life ☆☆☆
You'll play this game again. It's easy to remember and execute.

The game in more detail
Circulate a four pint jug (or smaller if playing with only a few players). Each player must contribute some or all of their personal drink to fill the communal jug. This is then called[7] the Challenge.

The Challenge is made!

Distribute the half pint glasses, one to each player. Each players glass is then filled from the Challenge. Don't worry if there is some drink left over in the jug as this will be distributed later.

There are two ways to play:

Option 1
The most straightforward way is for one player to drink their drink and initiate a game of 'Next!' (p9). Keep playing until all the Challenge has been drunk.

Option 2
You can play a game of 'higher and lower' using a pack of cards. The **go** passes in one direction around the table. Player 1 calls 'higher' or 'lower' and the **Administrator** turns over the top card. If the player's call is wrong they down their glass of the Challenge and then call again. The go

stays with Player 1 until he or she makes a correct call. When they get it right the go moves on.

INFO+ If the card turned over is of equal value to the one before this is neither 'higher' nor 'lower' and the player drinks.

You can make as many Challenges as you like. Challenge yourself to make the biggest Challenge you and your friends can handle. Remember — if you ever decide to play 'The Challenge' on your own, seek help!

Chapter 2
Gambling Games

 Four Aces

Brief description
The turn of cards decides who 'thinks of the drink', who 'pays for the drink', who 'gets the drink' and who 'drinks the drink'.

Number of players
Four players or more.

Situation
A bar or pub.

Drinks needed
Buying drinks is part of the game. See below.

Difficulty
Easy

Intoxication level
High

Implements needed
A pack of cards.

Shelf life ☆☆☆
Lasts as long as you've got the money to pay.

The game in more detail

This game is very easy but can cost a lot of money. You will need a shuffled pack of cards placed face down. In turn the players take one card off the top. Aces are the only cards that matter and when one comes up, everyone must note who turned it.

The player who turns over the first ace 'thinks of the drink'. When the first ace has been turned over, the drink to be consumed *must be picked and agreed on before* any further cards are turned.

The player who turns over the second ace will be the one who goes to the bar and orders the drink at the end of the game. The player who turns the third ace pays for the drink at the bar. The player who pulls the fourth and final ace drinks the drink.

Once the fourth and final ace is pulled it's time to administer the drink. The drink is ordered (by the player who pulled the second ace), paid for (by the player who pulled the third ace) and drunk (by the player who turned the fourth ace).

You can decide on a standard 'baseline' amount for the fine in each **round**[2], e.g. three shots from the **top row (T)** 'topped off' with **beer** or cider. If the fine is too low then the fear of punishment will be missing and the game will not be as exciting. Everyone must have the ability to pay every time and this is why this drinking game is particularly prevalent in the armed forces, where spillage and mess bills are cheap and players enjoy the benefits of a considerable expendable income.

Spoof

Brief description
Players hold out one hand concealing one, two, three or no coins. Everyone then tries to guess the total number of coins presented by the group, or in 'Negative Team Spoof' to guess any number *but* the one presented.

Number of players
It is possible to play with two players, however the game is better suited to three or more players.

Situation
Once the game is learnt, it can be played in any drinking environment.

Drinks needed
If you are going **soft**, then it can be played with pints and one **finger** fines. If a slightly more **savage** game is required, then have **shorts**.

Difficulty
Easy

Intoxication level
Medium.
INFO+ Can be played in any state from sober right up to completely **lashed** (also **pissed**).

Implements needed
Three coins per person of any value.

Shelf life ☆☆☆☆
Although 'Spoof' in its most basic form is very simple, it is highly addictive.

The team on the right presents coins in 'Team Spoof'

Revealing coins (the Show) in 'Team Spoof'

The game in more detail

Each player has three coins. Each coin counts as 'one' and not its monetary face value. The game begins and each player holds the coins behind their back. Secretly they each decide how many coins to present in a closed fist to the group: either zero (known as 'Spoof'), one, two or three. Any coins not presented remain in a closed fist behind the back. The game is to guess the total number of coins presented by the group. For example, in a game with three players, the possible number of coins is 0,1,2,3,4,5,6,7,8 or 9.

No two players *can* **call**[2] the same number. So if you really want a certain number because you're a clairvoyant, get in quickly!

Tactically it is better to let other people reveal their number first. You may be able to roughly calculate how many coins each person has in their displayed fist by the prediction. However, hesitating or intentionally slow play is discouraged. Once every player has chosen their number, everyone opens their hands and the actual number of coins can be counted (see picture opposite).

To aid counting the procedure is to have each player, one by one, open their hand and say how many coins they have in it. Remember zero coins is said Spoof. If you have guessed the total number of coins correctly you are **out**[1] (which is a good thing). If no one gets the number, the game is repeated again and again until someone gets their prediction **spot on (S)**.

When someone goes out[1] for a correct prediction, the game restarts with one less player. This process is repeated until there is only one person remaining. The person left at the end is the loser and is fined. The fine must always be agreed upon before the game starts when all players still have the possibility of being the victim of the punishment. I suggest that the fine is quite **heavy** because the game takes some time to conclude.

Team Spoof
There are two ways of playing 'Team Spoof' – 'Nearest To' and 'Nearest To Negative'. The flip of a coin decides which is the 'guessing team' and which is the 'presenting team'. It is better to be 'guessers' in 'Nearest to Negative Team Spoof' and presenters in 'Nearest To Team Spoof'.

Nearest To Team Spoof
This type of 'Spoof' is known as 'Nearest To' because not only are you aiming to get the prediction spot on, but also to avoid the fines that apply when you are one or more coins away from a correct prediction.

It seems the guessers were victorious on this occasion

You can play with four, six, eight or more players.

Each team must have the same number, i.e. for a game with four players there will be two on each side.

In this game you can collude with your team mate(s) as to how many coins you're going to **put in (P)** as a team.

The fining is also different in 'Team Spoof'. You are still trying to guess the number of coins presented **on the nose (N)**. However, if you do not get it right, then the discrepancy will be the number of fingers each member of your team is fined.

For example, if your team of two selected three as your guess and the amount of coins the other team presented was six, you would have been three coins out from the answer. You are fined three fingers each.

The presenting team continues to present until the guessers make a correct guess. When this happens the presenting team must finish their drinks as the fine for losing the **power**. The new presenting team will then be required to 'refresh' the new guessers' drinks in order to try and win back the power.

In this type of 'Team spoof', the presenters are said to be the 'bullies' of the guessers.

Nearest To Negative Team Spoof

Again you need four, six, eight or more players with equal numbers on each side.

This is just a different way of finding winners and losers. The guessing team has to try and guess any number *other* than the number the presenting team has in their fists. The fines are imposed on the presenting team and the guessing team can bully their adversaries. As long as the guessing team avoid guessing the exact number of coins presented, they can keep making the presenters drink fines. The presenters' fine is the number of coins they were away from trapping the guessers to the exact number converted into fingers.

For example if the presenters put in six and the guessers said four, the fine for the presenters will be two fingers for every team member.

In this type of 'Team Spoof' the guessers are said to be the 'bullies' of the presenters.

Arrogance

Brief description
On your **go** you must first make a contribution to a communal glass. This can be as much or as little drink as you like. You then flip either one or two coins depending on whether you are playing 'One Coin Arrogance' or 'Two Coin Arrogance'. If the wrong result comes up you will have to drink — the chances of you drinking or not drinking on any one go are 50:50.

Number of players
Playing with two players is possible but four plus is best. You don't want more than eight players.

Situation
'Two Coin Arrogance' is best instigated in a **pre-lash (P)** situation but 'One Coin Arrogance' can be played almost anywhere.

Drinks needed
Anything you're drinking. It is beneficial for the **mix** if people are drinking different drinks. This will ensure that the communal glass will have become an evil concoction, i.e. something like a **dirty pint (D)**.

Difficulty
Medium

INFO+ 'One Coin Arrogance' (i.e. the basic game) is very easy. 'Two Coin Arrogance' is of medium difficulty, but gets increasingly difficult to play as players add new rules.

Intoxication level
High

INFO+ Arrogant sadistic players will play as though this is **Russian Roulette (R)** making the **stakes** high every time. In the end everyone gets completely **wrecked**!

Implements needed
One coin or two and an empty pint glass or larger vessel for contributions.

Shelf life ☆☆☆☆☆

A true classic! In my top five best games for pre-lash as this is highly addictive and great fun.

The game in more detail

There are two versions of this game. We'll start with the basic 'One Coin Arrogance' and graduate to the more fun 'Two Coin Arrogance'. First decide which way the game will move; left or right round the circle. Once the direction is selected, the go will always move one player at a time in this direction, ensuring every player has a go. See 'Two Tails' under 'Two Coin Arrogance' below for the only exception to this rule. The game is continuous and does not stop after a specific number of **rounds**[2]. Stop the game when you become sick of it, or as is more likely to be the case, when you become sick from the alcohol (although if you are truly **savage, bundering**[1] or a **tactical bunder (B²)**, should not stop your **lash**!).

One Coin Arrogance
Contributing

Before your go and on any subsequent go, you must make a contribution to the communal glass. Your contribution can be as much or as little as you like.

Flip/call[1]

Flip a single coin and predict how it will land (either heads or tails) while it is in the air.

Correct prediction

If you win on your go (i.e. make the right prediction), you do not have to drink and the vessel will pass to the next player.

Wrong prediction

However if you lose on your go (i.e. make the wrong prediction) you will drink everything in the communal glass.

To be or not to be arrogant? That is the question

In 'One Coin Arrogance' you have a 50:50 chance of success or failure. Your own arrogance and belief that you will succeed will determine how much you contribute to the glass.

Pro-arrogance
They say 'fortune favours the brave'.

If you are particularly confident or arrogant, you'll want to contribute lots of your drink in the expectation that you will get the coin flip correct. If you are correct you'll have the added satisfaction of seeing the person next to you have to take their go with the risk of having to drink what you have contributed to the communal cup or **pot**.

Against arrogance
Being arrogant can backfire and your arrogance might lead to you drinking the hefty contribution you made. Bullet in the foot anyone?

Building the pot
If the **call**[2] is made correctly on successive players' goes, then the communal drink will build. This adds tension to the flip and call[2] on each successive go. It can be particularly exciting if a run of correct calls[2] happen, and players are drinking different drinks as this will lead to the formation of a horrendous dirty pint.

This game is all about wanting to **stitch up (S)** your mates. Therefore I say be arrogant!

Two Coin Arrogance
As the name suggests, two coins are used on the flip. No prediction is made. Instead the player drinks or doesn't drink depending on what combination of coins the flip brings. There is still a 50:50 chance you will have to drink on your go, but as new rules are added in the course of the game you may be forced to drink more than your fair share of bad luck!

One of each
A tail and a head, or head and tail in 'Two Coin Arrogance' means the player must drink the contents of the communal vessel. You then pass the empty pot to the next player to have a go.

One head, one tail — drink the contents of the communal pot and then pass the go and the empty pot on to the next player

Two heads — pass the go and the pot on to the next player

Two tails — make up a rule and then pass the go and the pot on to the next player

Two heads

Two heads passes the go to the player next to you like a correct call in 'One Coin Arrogance'.

Two tails

Two tails also passes on the go but in addition requires the player who flipped the two tails to make up a new rule. The rule created has to be adhered to by all players for the rest of the game, unless a player uses a subsequent tail flip to overturn the earlier (and apparently unpopular) rule.

Some traditional 'Arrogance' rules
- on receiving the pot, the player must nod their head. If they forget then they are fined. (You can replace the nod with any action or sound. The passing and receiving of the vessel is

one of the formalities of the game and the action will happen everytime the go moves on. The action will become part of the ceremony of the game and it is easy to notice if it is left out).

- no swearing (you will find this difficult once everyone has had a few drinks). Any expletives are fined.
- **no pointing (P)** with fingers, you'll be surprised how hard this is. Pointing with your elbow is acceptable and will be highly amusing.
- left-hand drinking (simple but effective). Anyone who drinks with their right hand has **buffaloed**. If you see this happen **call**[4] **"Buffalo!"** and the offending player will be fined.

Changing rules

Use your imagination and make up your own rules. There might be someone really loud at the table so your rule could be that the player is not allowed to talk for the duration of the game (very anti-social but quite funny!). A rule created can be over-ruled by another rule. If the person who has been silenced gets two tails on their go, they could pass a new rule saying they are allowed to talk. You cannot over-rule a rule and also make up a new rule on the same go. Rules are like wishes: you can't recall them but you can over-rule them if you have another wish. So use them wisely in the first place!

The breaking of rules

If a rule is broken, then the contribution vessel passes directly and immediately to that player no matter whose go it is or what is taking place in the game. The guilty party then has to drink the contents of the communal vessel **in one (O)** (i.e. **down** or **chin**) and then it is their go, i.e. they must contribute and then flip. Once they have done this, the go continues to circulate in the normal way.

Fives

Brief description
An open hand counts as five. A closed hand counts as zero. Players stand in a circle. All at the same time they put their right hand into the circle, either open or closed. At the same moment, the player whose **go** it is makes their **call**[2]. In a four-player game the call could be 'zero', 'five', 'ten', 'fifteen' or 'twenty'. Anyone who guesses correctly goes **out**[1]. The last player in loses and pays a heavy fine.

Number of players
You can play with two players, but don't have more than ten players on a 'single-handed' game and no more than six players on a 'double-handed' game.

Situation
You need to be able to hear the multiples of five as they are **called**[3]. Once you know the game you can play it pretty much anywhere. Beware! This game is really addictive.

Drinks needed
Any

Difficulty
Medium

INFO+ It is reasonably difficult to learn 'Fives'. However, this game is completely logical. Certain people tend to pick it up quicker than others.

Intoxication level
Low

Implements needed
None

Shelf life ☆☆☆☆☆

You'll play 'Fives' when you're at the airport, on the train or in the park, literally anywhere as long as you're with someone else. Even blasphemously without a drink! This is a game I really enjoy and highly recommend, **a great (G)!**

The game in more detail

This is an even better game than **Paper, Scissors, Stone (P)** for making decisions.

e.g. "**Bagsy** not taking out the rubbish! Right, a game of 'Fives' to decide then, with a gun start." See below under 'For **veterans**'.

The beginners' way

I must stress that the beginners' way is not the best way to play! I would suggest that you do not play this version but that you only learn it in order to pick up the basic idea of the game. The beginners' version presents the crucial ideas simply, whereas the advanced version can easily be picked up once the basic principles of the beginners' version are understood. In 'Fives' the go always moves to the left round the circle.

Single-handed beginners' 'Fives'

Every player uses one hand. The other hand is placed behind the back or by the side. The hand can either show a five (an open hand) or a zero (a closed fist) on a **show**. A show is when someone makes a guess. You mustn't tell anyone what you intend to show. The idea of the game is to guess on your go the correct sum total offered into the circle by all players. In a four-player game this could be 'zero', 'five', 'ten', 'fifteen' or 'twenty'. With six players the combinations would also include 'twenty-five' and 'thirty'.

On a go you could all say "One, two, three!" and mark the beat with closed fists just as in 'Paper, Scissors, Stone'. This helps everyone to show their five or zero at the same time, i.e. on the fourth beat. At the same time the player whose go it is makes their guess.

Going out
Exit sentence

If you guess correctly and the hands put in by the other players add up to your guess, then say "Thank you very much, ladies and gentlemen, for a lovely game of Fives!". It doesn't matter if it's all males or all females playing, you still say 'ladies and gentlemen'. You can make up your own exit sentence if you like but there must be an exit sentence.

No celebration
Before, during and after saying the exit sentence, you must not celebrate or smile, the sentence must be deadpan. We're talking about a mixture of **Jimmy Carr (C)** and **Jack Dee (D)** be delivered. If you do smile, laugh or celebrate, with a "Yes!" for example, you are back in the game and it's the next person's go.

An example game
In this game there are six players with one hand, so the maximum call[2] is 30 (everyone puts out their open hand) and the minimum is zero (everyone puts in a fist):

INFO+ On each **round**[2] of 'Fives', hands must be put in at exactly the same time as the caller makes their guess.

Player 1: "One, two, three... ten." (open hand — five)

Player 2: (five)

Player 3: (zero)

Player 4: (five)

Player 5: (five)

Player 6: (zero)

The total equals 20 (see photo on next page) so the guess was wrong and the game continues to the left.

The go is with Player 1 who guessed "Ten" but they were wrong as the total adds up to 20

Player 1: (five)

Player 2: (zero)

Player 3: (zero)

Player 4: (zero)

Player 5: (zero)

Player 6: "One, two, three… twenty" (five)

The go is with Player 6 who guessed "Twenty", however the total is 10

The total is ten so the game continues.

Player 1: (five)

Player 2: (five)

Player 3: (zero)

Player 4: (zero)

Player 5: "One two three… fifteen"(five)

Player 6: (zero)

The go is with Player 5 who guesses "Fifteen". They are correct! With the correct exit sentence, Player 5 will be out[1]

Player 5 sees the total is correct at 15, so says, "Thank you very much, ladies and gentlemen, for a lovely game of Fives". Player 5 is now out[1].

Player 1: (zero)

Player 2: (zero)

Player 3: (zero)

Player 4: "One, two, three… ten" (five)

Player 6: (zero)

The total equals five so the game continues.

Player 1: (zero)

Player 2: (zero)

Player 3: "One, two, three… zero" (zero)

Player 4: (zero)

Player 6: (zero)

The go is with Player 3 who says "Zero". They are correct! With the correct exit sentence, Player 3 will be out[1] too

The total was 0, so Player 3 was correct. She says the exit sentence correctly and goes out[1].

Player 1: (five)

Player 2: "One, two, three… ten" (zero)

Player 4: (five)

Player 6: (zero)

The total was 10 so Player 2 was correct. With the exit sentence said, Player 2 goes out[1].

We're now back to Player 1, with only 3 players left in the game.

Player 1: "One, two, three… five" (zero)

Player 4: (zero)

Player 6: (zero)

The go is with Player 1 who says "Five", however the total is zero

The total was 0 so the game continues.

Player 1: (zero)

Player 4: (five)

Player 6: "One, two, three... five" (zero)

The go is with Player 6 who says "Five". They are correct! Player 6 will be out[1] if they say the exit sentence, but will they be able to resist celebrating?

The total was 5 but due to the tension, Player 6 celebrates with a little smile and thus is back in the game.

Player 1: (zero)

Player 4: "One, two, three... ten" (five)

Player 6: (five)

The total was 10 so Player 4 goes out[1].

Player 1: "One, two, three... ten" (five)

Player 6: (five)

The go is with Player 1 who says "Ten". They are correct! With the correct exit sentence, Player 1 will be out[1].

Player 1 won! He holds back the urge to celebrate and says the exit sentence. Player 6 is now fined heavily for losing!

Double-handed beginners' 'Fives'

Played in exactly the same way as single-handed 'Fives' but you've more hands in the game and fewer players are needed. On the guess you can put in a five hand and a zero fist (five), two fives (ten) or two fists (zero).

A five and a zero   A double-handed five   A double-handed zero

When you guess the sum total of the hands correctly you take one hand out[1] and say the exit sentence. You play on with the single hand. The maximum total drops by five. In a change to the one-handed version it is now your start (see below under 'The right to restart'). The second time you get the guess correct followed by the correct exit sentence, you are out[1] because you have won on both hands.

The right to restart
When you guess the sum total of the hands correctly, you take one hand out[1] and play on with the single hand. Instead of the go moving to the next player you get the chance to get your other hand out[1] by restarting the game.

I'll show you a quick example with four players to demonstrate the rule surrounding 'The right to restart'. The maximum 'in' is potentially forty, i.e. four players each putting in two hands as fives:

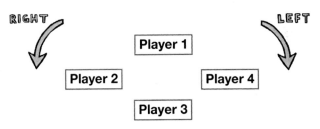

Player 1: (ten)

Player 2: "One, two, three… twenty" (five)

Player 3: (zero)

Player 4: (zero)

The *go* is with Player 2 who says "Twenty", however the total is 15

The total was 15 so the game continues to the left.

Player 1: "One, two, three... twenty-five" (ten)

Player 2: (ten)

Player 3: (zero)

Player 4: (five)

The go is with Player 1 who says "Twenty-five". They are correct! With the correct exit sentence, Player 1 can take one hand out[1]

After a quick count-up Player 1 realises that they are out[1], exits with the sentence and takes one hand out[1]. Player 1 now has the right to restart the game.

Player 1: "One, two, three... ten" (zero)

Player 2: (five)

Player 3: (five)

Player 4: (zero)

Player 1 realises that they have been lucky and won, and successfully says the exit sentence. They take their remaining hand away and are now out[1] of the game. The remaining players carry on.

Now I'll show you the correct and much better way to play, 'The advanced version!'. This is a non-stop version with better flow, which is more exciting and skilful. Please don't leave your knowledge at just the beginners' version of single and double handed 'Fives'.

Single-handed advanced 'Fives': First difference

Gone is the "one, two, three...guess". Instead you start a game by counting in multiples of five to the maximum amount in the game, i.e. if there are six in the game it would start "Five, ten, fifteen, twenty, twenty-five, thirty... guess". You still bob your fist as in Paper, Scissors, Stone to get the timing right.

So a start could go:

Player 1: "Five, ten, fifteen, twenty, twenty-five, thirty... ten."

Single-handed advanced 'Fives': Second difference

If a player guesses incorrectly the game does not restart. Instead the next player is allowed to immediately say their guess. To illustrate this **check out (C²)** the following:

Player 1: "Five, ten, fifteen, twenty, twenty-five, thirty... ten."

The total wasn't 10 so the game continues with the player to the left.

Player 6: "Fifteen."

It's not 15 so the game continues.

Player 5: "Twenty."

On the guess call you can change your hand. You do not remove your hand from the circle. You simply open or close your hand at the same moment as the call. This way the total keeps changing and the game is able to flow.

In this version of 'Fives' the game moves much faster. If you don't instantly recognise you've won, the game will move on when the next player calls. If you miss out and do not have time to say the exit sentence, they you'll miss your chance and have to **bite your lip (B)** and carry on playing. The saying is **"You snooze, you lose (S)!"** Making an exit call out of turn results in a fine so brush up your five times table. You'll find the more you play the quicker you get at working out the total.

For veterans

Gun starts are a way to take command of the go. Practice 'Fives' before you bring this rule in!

When a game of 'Fives' is proposed, any player can call[1] a gun start. This means that you're with players who have played before, i.e. **veterans**. Veteran players will realise the advantage of going first, i.e. you get a chance to be out[1] straightaway.

To do a gun start you say "Gun start!" and place the end of your thumb in the thumbs up position in the middle of your forehead.

Player 2 grabs the go with a gun start!

A gun start can also be called if someone repeatedly **messes up (M)** the start. By saying 'gun start' in this situation you're literally telling the player making the mistake, "You're not fit to start the game so give the **power** to me."

A gun start is not used if someone has gone out of the game (i.e. won) or if they have to rejoin the game after celebrating during the exit sentence. In these cases the go always moves to the left.

Be careful in your use of the gun start for you might have no right to take the go.

Therefore, to summarise, a gun start grabs the go when there is no starter at the beginning of the game, or if someone is messing up the start call (usually repeatedly before you have the right to take the start from them).

An example game of single-handed advanced 'Fives' with seven players:

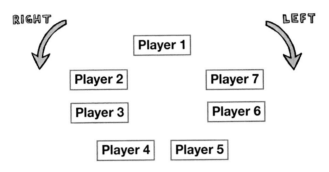

Player 1: (five)

Player 2: (five)

Player 3: (zero)

Player 4: (zero)

Player 5: "Gun start... five, ten, fifteen, twenty, twenty-five, thirty, thirty-five... twenty." (five)

Player 6: (zero)

Player 7: (zero)

The go is with Player 5 due to their 'gun start'. Player 5 says "Twenty", however the total is 15

The total is 15 so the game continues.

Player 1: (five)

Player 2: (five)

Player 3: (zero)

Player 4: "Thirty." (zero)

Player 5: (five)

Player 6: (five)

Player 7: (zero)

The total is 20 so the game continues.

Player 1: (five)

Player 2: (five)

Player 3: "Five." (five)

Player 4: (five)

Player 5: (five)

Player 6: (five)

Player 7: (zero)

The total is 30 so the game continues.

Player 1: (zero)

Player 2: "Zero." (zero)

Player 3: (zero)

Player 4: (zero)

Player 5: (zero)

Player 6: (zero)

Player 7: (zero)

After a quick glance, Player 2 says the exit sentence. Player 2 is now out[1].

Player 1: "Five, ten, fifteen, twenty, twenty-five, thirty… fifteen." (five)

Player 3: (five)

Player 4: (zero)

Player 5: (zero)

Player 6: (five)

Player 7: (zero)

The go is with Player 1 who says "Fifteen". They are correct! With the correct exit sentence, Player 1 will be out[1]

After a quick glance, Player 1 says the exit sentence. Player 1 is now out[1].

Player 7: "Five, fifteen, twenty, err… I mean five, ten… **fuck[1]!**"

Player 4: "Right… gun start!" (Player 4 has every right to take the start as Player 7 was making a mess).

Player 3: (five)

Player 4: "Five, ten, fifteen, twenty, twenty-five… twenty." (five)

Player 5: (zero)

Player 6: (five)

Player 7: (five)

After a quick count up, Player 4 remembers to say the exit sentence straightfaced. Player 4 is now out[1].

Player 3: "Five, ten, fifteen, twenty… twenty." (five)

Player 5: (zero)

Player 6: (five)

Player 7: (five)

This game would continue until there is a loser. Just remember, if you have to start, just count up to the number of fives that are in and then make your guess. It's easy and logical!

Double-handed advanced 'Fives'
As I've said already, double-handed 'Fives' is exactly the same but there are more hands in the game so fewer players are needed. On the guess you can therefore put in a five and a zero fist (five), two fives (ten) or two fists (zero) (see p38). Important! You must remember that even though you have two hands you only get one call[2] on your go unless (see 'The right to restart' below) you manage to get the call[2] right and so get the chance to restart the game.

When you guess the sum total of the hands correctly you take one hand out[1] after saying "Thank you very much, ladies and gentlemen, for a lovely game of Fives!". You now have the right to restart.

The right to restart
When you guess the sum total of the hands correctly you take one hand out[1] and play on with the single hand (the maximum sum total will have dropped by five). Instead of the go moving to the next player you get the chance to get your other hand out[1] by restarting the game.

I'll show you a quick example with four players to demonstrate the rule surrounding 'The right to restart'. The maximum in is potentially 40, i.e. four players each putting in both their hands as five.

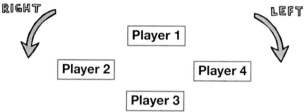

Player 1: (ten)

Player 2: "Five, ten, fifteen, twenty, twenty five, thirty, thirty-five, forty...
            twenty." (five)

Player 3: (zero)

Player 4: (zero)

The go is with Player 2 who says "Twenty", however the total is 15

The total was 15 so the game continues to the left.

Player 1: "Fifteen." (five)

Player 2: (five)

Player 3: (five)

Player 4: (zero)

After a quick count-up, Player 1 realises that they got the total correct, exit with the correct sentence and takes one hand out[1]. Player 1 now starts again.

Player 1: "Five, ten, fifteen, twenty, twenty-five, thirty, thirty-five… twenty." (five)

Player 2: (five)

Player 3: (ten)

Player 4: (zero)

Player 1 realises that they have been lucky and won. They say the exit sentence and takes out their remaining hand. Player 1 is now out[1] of the game, leaving the remaining players to play on.

Master of the Three

a.k.a Three Man or Pigeon

Brief description
Depending on the roll of the two dice, either a rule is made up or certain player(s) will be required to drink. If someone is unlucky enough to be a 'Master of the Three' they will be drinking considerably more than everyone else. Watch out for the dangerous number '8'. You'll come to anticipate this number with fear!

Number of players
Three players or more.

Situation
A great **pre-lash (P)** game. This game originated as a game played by Spanish teenagers on the streets with a cola and wine mix.

Drinks needed
If you want to be traditional, then mix half cola with half cheap red wine. This is **called**[7] many things, including Kailmotxo, Bambus and Korea. However, any drink will suffice.

Difficulty
Easy
INFO+ The rules are very straightforward.

Intoxication level
High

Implements needed
You will need a pair of dice and enough half/small glasses for everyone playing. Try to make everyones' glasses the same size. You may also need something to roll the dice in to so they don't go flying everywhere.

Shelf life ☆☆☆☆
This will last a long time and you'll return to this game again.

Rule number one

Nobody is allowed to say the word 'drink'. You can refer to it as 'the D word' or 'D-R-I-N-K'. Other helpful alternatives are 'consume', '**chin** it' or 'take some of that alcoholic beverage'. See **unmentionable words (U)** for more details.

Rule number two

On your **go**, you must ensure that everyone playing has a full glass *before* rolling any dice.

Notice that everyone has a similar-sized drink, all within reach of the players

If you fail to do so you will be fined a **finger**. You'll see that it's in your interest to ensure that everyone drinks the same, especially if the dreaded '8' is rolled. This rule is crucial to ensure fairness.

The deciding one die roll a.k.a a roll off

Sit in a group, either on the floor or round a table. Everyone rolls *one* dice in turn before the game starts properly. This decides who starts first (the highest roll) and importantly who, if anyone, will be a 'Master of the Three'. *Any threes that are rolled at this point must be remembered.* Any player who rolls a three is called[7] a 'Master of the Three'. The player with the highest roll will start. If there is more than one player with the highest roll, have another **roll-off (R)**.

How to play
The player who won the one dice roll-off to start goes first. They now pick up *both* dice. Roll the dice so everyone can see the result, i.e. into the centre of the group.

It's the total score that counts, i.e. three and four scores seven, except in a couple of special situations explained below.

The rule on doubles
If a double is rolled, the roller can distribute the value in fingers as a fine (i.e. if a double four is rolled they have four fingers to distribute). If two twos are rolled, then the roller can give out two fingers as a fine to another player(s). The roller decides how to distribute the fines. In the example of the two twos, they could give out one finger to one player, one finger to another or both fingers to one player.

Master of the Three
INFO+ Anyone unlucky enough to roll a three in the initional roll-off becomes 'Master of the Three'. There can be more than one 'Master of the Three'. There also might be no 'Master of the Three'.

The creation of 3
Any three on any single dice means a one finger fine for a 'Master of the Three'. 'Masters of the Three' also drink when the total on the dice is three (i.e. one and two) and when a six is rolled (it counts as two threes).

The creation of 7
The combinations to make a 7 are a 3-4, 1-6 and 2-5. All these result in a one finger fine for the player to the *left* of whoever rolled.

The creation of 9
The combinations to make a 9 are 3-6 and 4-5. All these result in a one finger fine for the player to the *right* of whoever rolled.

Make up your own rules
A good idea is to make up a rule for a currently unused number such as 4 or 5. As with all rules, a rule can be used to cancel a previously-

created unpopular rule. A rule cannot be used to tamper with the basics of the game, i.e. the rule on scoring a 7 or a 9 for instance, or the 'Master of the Three' rule.

The creation of 8
The combinations to make an 8 are 5-3, 6-2 and 4-4. This is the dreaded roll! If an '8' is rolled then all players must **down** their drinks as fast as possible and bang their finished glass down on the table. The last person to do this will be fined another whole drink.

Both the rules on 'doubles' and the 'Master of the Three' operate alongside the rules above, i.e. 7, 8, 9 and 11. Therefore one roll can have many consequences.

For example, if a 7 is made with a 3-4, then the 'Creation of 7' is implemented and, because of the presence of a 3, so is the 'Master of the Three' rule.

To make this game work you *must* stick to the very structured rules!

Chapter 3
Circle Go Games

'Yee-ha!'

a.k.a. 'Zoom, Bounce, Bong'

Brief description
Use a variety of Wild West inspired-signals to send the **go** round the group. Different signals move the go on in different ways.

Number of players
More than four players.

Situation
Loud drinking **session** where you're not afraid to look silly.

Drinks needed
Any

Difficulty
Medium

Intoxication level
Medium

Implements needed
None

Shelf life ☆☆☆
Won't last for ever, but will entertain for some time before it loses its spark.

The game in more detail

This was one of the first drinking games I learnt and it is a typical **circle go game (C)**, where the go is passed around the circle with sounds and signals.

You can create your own signals but commonly used ones are:

Action 1 — Yee-ha
Say: "Yee-ha!" (like a cowboy).

Action: Bring one arm across your chest as though you are doing a boxing hook but with your elbow tucked in. If the go is coming from your left, you use your right arm and hook across your body to the left. If the go is coming from the right use your left arm and hook across yourself to the right.

'Yee-ha' moving the go right, right arm hooking across the body

What does it do?
Sends the go on to the next player without changing the direction.

Action 2 — Hoedown
Say: "Hoedown!" (like a Native American Indian).

Action: Raise your left or right arm depending on the direction of play. Hold the arm out with elbow in line with shoulder and create a 90° angle between your bicep and forearm. Your fist should be closed. The action should look like one half of a boxing guard. If the go is coming from your left you should be using your right arm to 'block' and reverse the go. Therefore, if the go is coming from your right, use your left arm.

Hoedown with the go coming from Player 4 right. Notice the left arm is used by Player 3 to 'block' the go back

What does it do?
Reverses the direction of play and sends the go back one place to the player directly to your left or right.

Action 3 — Haybarn
Say: "Haybarn!"

Action: Make a roof (like a Pizza Hut sign) over your head.

Haybarn

What does it do?

Moves the go back to the player who started the game. Play continues in the same direction it was going when it came to the 'Haybarn' **caller**[1]. They must think carefully about which arm to raise if they intend to use a 'Yee-ha' or 'Hoedown' call[1]. See the example games below for a description of how this works in practice.

Action 4 — Giddy up

Say: "Giddy up!"

Action: Pretend to thrash the reins on a horse with both hands.

Giddy up — thrash those reins like you mean it!

What does it do?

Makes the go skip one player. The direction of play does not change.

INFO+ 'Giddy up' is a easy call[1] to make as unlike the 'Yee-ha' and 'Hoedown' calls it does not matter which arm you use.

Action 5 — Milk the cow

INFO+ This call[1] is optional but you could introduce this or similar a call[1] after everyone has mastered the basics.

Say: "Milk the cow!"

Action: Pretend to milk those teats.

What does it do?
Reverses the direction of the go and skips a go.

**Milk the cow — move your hands up and down
like you are milking cow teats**

Starting the game
The best way to introduce complete amateurs is to start with only one
call[1], 'Yee-ha'. As the Starter, you would say "A game of 'Yee-ha!' to my
left... yee-ha!" The game will then pass around all the players. Each one
crooks their right arm, says "Yee-ha!" and passes the go on to the left.
Play for a while with both 'Yee-ha' and 'Hoedown' in circulation and then
introduce 'Giddy up'. Once all players seem to have the idea of these
three calls, introduce 'Haybarn', 'Milk the cow' and so on.

Example game using all calls[1]:

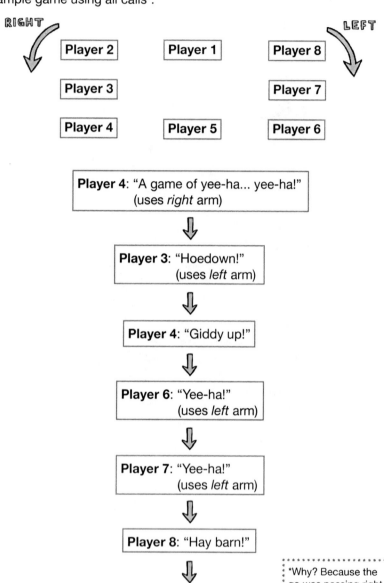

RIGHT

LEFT

Player 2	Player 1	Player 8
Player 3		Player 7
Player 4	Player 5	Player 6

Player 4: "A game of yee-ha... yee-ha!"
(uses *right* arm)

⬇

Player 3: "Hoedown!"
(uses *left* arm)

⬇

Player 4: "Giddy up!"

⬇

Player 6: "Yee-ha!"
(uses *left* arm)

⬇

Player 7: "Yee-ha!"
(uses *left* arm)

⬇

Player 8: "Hay barn!"

⬇

Player 4: "Hoedown!"
(uses *right* arm)*

*Why? Because the go was passing right from Player 7 to 8. So Player 4 continues as though he or she had just received the go from their right.

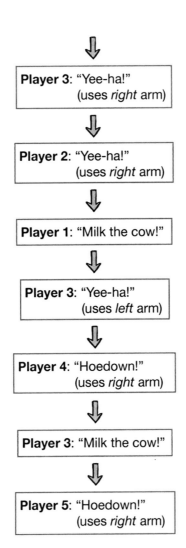

Player 3: "Yee-ha!"
(uses *right* arm)

Player 2: "Yee-ha!"
(uses *right* arm)

Player 1: "Milk the cow!"

Player 3: "Yee-ha!"
(uses *left* arm)

Player 4: "Hoedown!"
(uses *right* arm)

Player 3: "Milk the cow!"

Player 5: "Hoedown!"
(uses *right* arm)

Errors and fines

The game above is a model game providing an example of how to play. You are unlikely to play a game with such an error-free sequence.

Any **mess up (M)** requires a fine of a **finger** of drink.

Fines should be imposed for:
- going out of turn

- doing the wrong action for the call[1]
- using the wrong arm for a 'Hoedown' or 'Yee-ha' (the most frequently fined mistake).

This is the wrong arm for a 'Yee-ha!' call when the go is travelling in this direction

Restarting

The player directly to the left of the player who messed up should start. The way to call this is "Left of the **fuck-up**[3] starts!" Another useful phrase is "**A quick game's a good game (Q)**", e.g. "A quick game's a good game, left of the fuck-up if you please!" This keeps the game moving quickly. You'll probably find that the fuck-up, i.e. the person who messed up last time, might be too occupied with their fine to realise the game has restarted and this may mean they become a **repeat offender (R)**. All very amusing!

A word on starts

The 'Yee-ha' arm action shows the direction in which the game will **move off (M)** so it's not really necessary to say "A game of 'Yee-ha!' to my left…" or "A game of 'Yee-ha!' to my right…" You can also "Haybarn" to yourself although this is really quite pointless as it will be your go again immediately!

Now I'll show you an example of a more realistic game with mistakes and how it is played out:

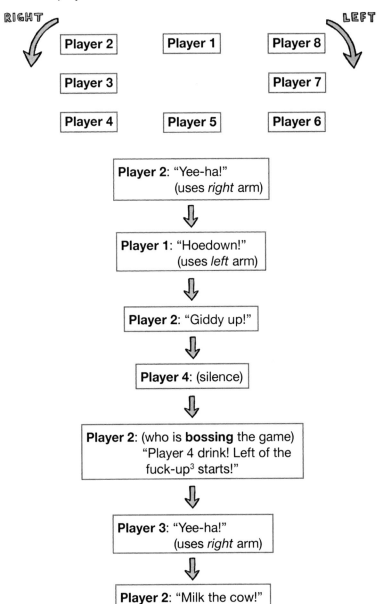

Player 4: "Haybarn!"

Player 2: "Yee-ha!"
(uses *left* arm)*

Player 3: "Giddy up!"

Player 5: "Hoedown!"
(uses *right* arm)

*Why? Because Player 3 said "Yee-ha!" moving the go left to Player 2 who reversed the go and skipped a player with a "Milk the cow" to Player 4, so now the go is moving right. Player 4 said "Haybarn" which returned the go to the starter (Player 2) with the direction of the go coming from the right.

Player 4: (silence)
Player 2: (who is bossing the game)
    "Player 4 drink! Left of the fuck-up[3] starts!"

Player 3: "Yee-ha!"
(uses *left* arm)

Player 4: "Haybarn!"

Player 2: "Hoedown!"
(uses *right* arm)**

**Why? Because the go moved right from Player 3 to 4 and thus was moving to the right around the circle. Player 2's 'Hoedown' sends the go back to the left, to Player 1.

Player 1: (silence)
Player 2: "Player 1 drink! Left of the fuck-up[3] starts!"

Using your eyes

When you are good at this game, you will notice that you can use your eyes to put people off. You'll be surprised how many inexperienced players will think it's their go if you use a call[1] that sends the go away from them, but still look them convincingly in the eye.

Ping-Pang-Pong

Brief description

The **go** is passed around the circle *to the left* using the **calls**[1] 'Ping', 'Pang' and 'Pong'. 'Ping' and 'Pang' pass the go to the player immediately to your left. On a 'Pong' you make eye contact with any other player as you say 'Pong' to pass the go to them. You can also use eye contact on a 'Ping' or 'Pang' call to confuse other players about where the go is meant to be going. In theory you can just pay attention to eye contact on the 'Pong' call but this is easier said than done!

Number of players

At least four players. This is a big group game, so around ten is perfect.

Situation

You need to be able to hear what others are saying. The game is usually played when you are sat round a table with loads of friends.

Drinks needed

Any

Difficulty
Medium

Intoxication level
Medium

Implements needed

None

Shelf life ☆☆☆☆☆

You are in for a treat. I love this game, and it is **S.O.P.** for me at parties.

The game in more detail

Gather in a circle. Everyone needs to be able to see the eyes of every other player. Clearly explain that the go *always* passes to the left. This is important because as you will see (in 'Example game 2' below) there are tactics you can use to try and trick novice players into thinking the game will **move off (M)** right.

Player 3 has made an error. The go always moves left. Eye contact only matters on 'Pong'

To begin, the first player says "Ping" the player to their immediate left says "Pang" and the player to his or her left says "Pong". At the same time he or she looks into the eyes of *any other player*. They are only allowed to look at *one* player. Every player should be ready to receive a 'look', i.e. they should be looking at the "Pong" caller. Whoever receives the 'look' receives the 'go'. They say "Ping" and the go will then move off to their left.

'Ping', 'Pang' and 'Pong' calls¹ always move to the left

Player 8 then makes eye contact with any other player and the go will start on "Ping" with this player.

The go moves via eye contact from Player 8 who is 'Pong' to Player 5 who will be the new 'Ping'

This might sound hard but it really is an easy game to learn.

Example game 1:

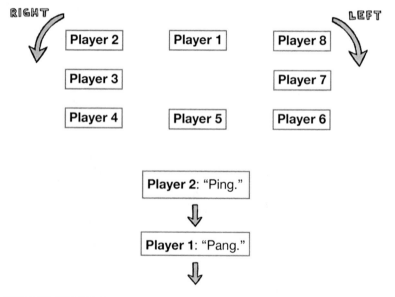

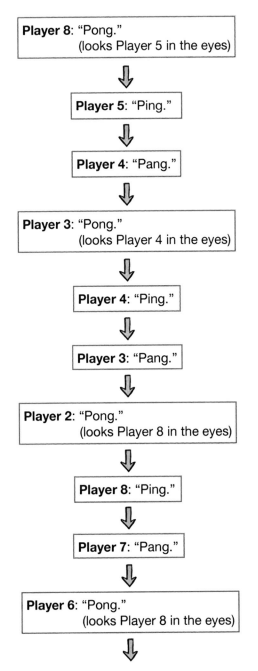

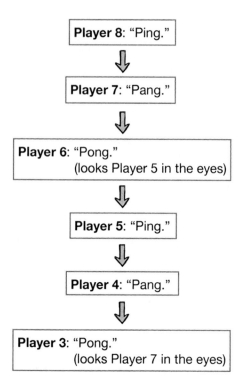

Hope you've got the idea. It's not rocket science!

Players are fined for:
- going out of turn
- not paying attention
- reacting too slowly.

It's up to you how much drink you fine, though I suggest one **finger** is adequate.

The game can either restart left of the **fuck-up**[3] or you can allow the person who **messed up (M)** to restart the game. It is acceptable to let someone who messed up restart in this game (unlike in most **circle go games (C)**) because a start is simply a "Ping" call[1] and thus the punished player will not slow down the game. The guilty party can **call**[3] "Ping," and then consume their finger. Nevertheless, the player being fined must remember to pay attention in case the "Pong" comes back to them. As with all circle games, keep the speed up. Remember the saying "**A quick game's a good game (Q)!**" and use it in this game.

Once players have mastered the basics as above, you should introduce them to the tactic of 'dummy' eye contact on "Ping" and "Pang" calls[1]. The game will then become rife with 'dummy' looks, which makes the game more interesting and will distinguish good players from merely average ones.

A word on starts
The game always moves off to the left. All you need to say is "Ping." However you can say "Ping-Pang-Pong to my right… Ping!" in order to try and trick the person to your right into making a mistake. Another tactic is to say "Ping," and look right (see the first photo in this game) or **double bluff (B)** it, by saying "Ping" and looking confidently in the eyes of the player to your left in the hope that it confuses them.

Now I'll show you an example game played by **veterans**. Note the amount of 'dummy' looks involved in the game.

Example game 2:

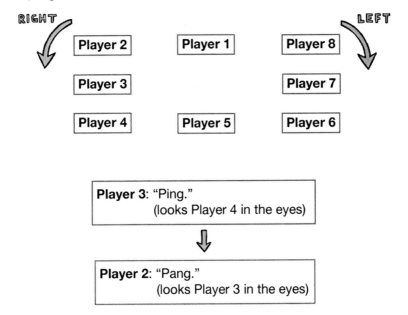

RIGHT

LEFT

| Player 2 | Player 1 | Player 8 |

| Player 3 | | Player 7 |

| Player 4 | Player 5 | Player 6 |

Player 3: "Ping."
(looks Player 4 in the eyes)

Player 2: "Pang."
(looks Player 3 in the eyes)

Player 1: "Pong."
(looks Player 7 in the eyes)

Player 7: "Ping."
(looks Player 8 in the eyes)

Player 6: "Pang."
(looks Player 4 in the eyes)

Player 5: "Pong."
(looks Player 4 in the eyes)

Player 4: "Ping."
(looks Player 5 in the eyes)

Player 3: "Pang."
(looks Player 4 in the eyes)

Player 2: "Pong."
(looks Player 6 in the eyes)

Player 6: "Ping."
(looks Player 7 in the eyes)

End of example game 2.

Zoom, Schwartz, Pafigliano

Brief description
Move the **go** round a circle of friends using **calls**[1] and eye contact with other players. A **circle go game (C)** similar to 'Ping-Pang-Pong' (p64), only much harder.

Number of players
Four players or more.

Situation
Must be somewhere quiet in order that calls[1] can be heard. The calls[1] in this game can become louder when players battle with one another.

Drinks needed
Any

Difficulty
Hard

INFO+ Difficult to **get** the knack but once you understand you'll never forget. The game plays by very strict rules.

Intoxication level
Medium

INFO+ Even the most **veteran** players can still be caught out by 'Zoom, Schwartz, Pafigliano'. If there is a player who can't get their head around this game and is still stupid enough to keep playing, then you might as well class this game as 'extreme' for they will get fined heavily!

Implements needed
None

Shelf life ☆☆☆☆
Another **great**! You'll return to this game time and time again.

The game in more detail
A mix between 'Ping-Pang-Pong' and 'Yee-ha!' (p53).

The three calls[1] are:
Call 1 — Zoom
Say: "Zoom" (in a normal voice).

What does it do and what do you do? Say it and look into the eyes of the person who is to receive the go. Sometimes it is also accompanied by a double-handed point, though this is not essential. Everyone should help keep the game going by looking into the eyes of the player who has the go.

You can say **"Zoom"** to any player other than the player who sent the go to you — notice the zoom hands

The only person you can't say "Zoom" to is the person who 'zoomed' you — you can't **zoom a zoomer (Z)**. This is because to zoom a zoomer is a 'Schwartz' call[1] as you will see below. Please don't think 'What the **fuck**[1]?' at this point, it's really straightforward.

Check out (C²) the 'Schwartz' call[1].

Call 2 — Schwartz
Say: "Schwartz" (in an authoritarian German accent).

This apparently means 'black' in German. However instead of 'black' it should mean 'back' because that's what it does in the context of this game.

What does it do and what do you do? If you look in the eyes of the person who sent the go to you and say "Schwartz" it sends the go back to them.

Player 4 has received the go from Player 5. To return the go, Player 4 looks Player 5 in the eyes and says "Schwartz."

You can *only* "Schwartz" the player who sent you the go.

Call 3 — Pafigliano
Say: "Pafigliano" (in an Italian accent).

Player 4 can look at any player other than the player who sent them the go (in this case Player 5) and say "Pafigliano", returning it to Player 5.

What does it do and what do you do? A 'Pafigliano' is a 'dummy zoom' but behaves like a 'Schwartz'. This might sound complicated but it's not! Basically you look at anyone *but* the person who sent the go to you and say "Pafigliano".

The go will then return to the player who sent you the go. So a 'Pafigliano' moves the go like a 'Schwartz' but you use the eyes as in a 'Zoom'. That actually makes sense. I even surprised myself!

INFO+ You can get into battles with players where you and the other player 'Schwartz' and 'Pafigliano' back and forth. These are resolved when someone 'zooms out'.

Look at this example game and see if you can follow:

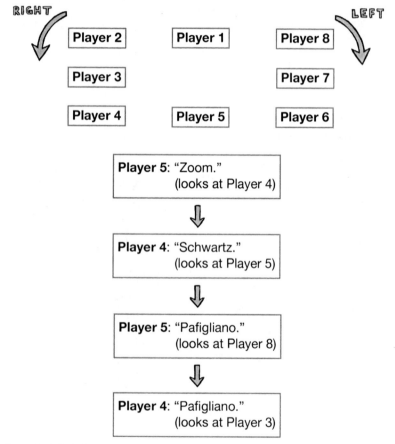

Player 5: "Zoom."
(looks at Player 1)

Player 1: "Zoom."
(looks at Player 2)

Player 2: "Schwartz."
(looks at Player 1)

Player 1: "Pafigliano."
(looks at Player 4)

Player 2: "Zoom."
(looks at Player 1) *Wrong!*
Player 5: "Player 2 drink! You can't say
'Zoom' to someone who
has sent you the go. **Left of
the fuck-up (F³)** starts.
Player 1 if you please..."

Player 1: "Zoom."
(looks at Player 5)

Player 5: "Schwartz."
(looks at Player 1)

> **Player 1:** "Pafigliano."
> (looks at Player 2)

> **Player 2:** "Zoom."
> (looks at Player 1) *Wrong!*
> **Player 5:** "Drink again Player 2! A 'Pafigliano' would
> return the go to me. **You're out of line (O).**
> Left of the fuck-up[3] starts!"

> **Player 1:** "Zoom."
> (looks at Player 8)

> **Player 8:** "Pafigliano."
> (looks at Player 6)

> **Player 1:** "Zoom."
> (looks at Player 6)

Fines

A fine applies to any mistake, e.g. wrong eye work, going out of turn, or mixing calls[1]. I usually play that a fine is one **finger**, though obviously it's up to you how **soft** or **hardcore** you fine.

A word on starts

Starts always begin on a 'Zoom' as it's impossible to start on any other call[1]. This game, like many of the other circle go games, relies on speed so I'd suggest that the left of the fuck-up[3] starts in order that the game doesn't halt for a player to take their fine. Also use the saying "**A quick game's a good game (Q)!**" to keep the speed up.

Sevens
a.k.a Bottle

Brief description
A counting game in which any number with a 7 in it (17, 27, etc.) or multiple of 7 (7, 14, 21, etc.) must not be mentioned. In place of the unmentionable 7, any other word can be used.

Number of players
Six players or more.

Situation
Pretty much any situation is fine. This is a harmless game although all players will be required to hear **calls**[1] so loud places are not suitable.

Drinks needed
Any

Difficulty
Easy
INFO+ Very easy to learn but as with all drinking games, tricky to play.

Intoxication level
Low

Implements needed
None

Shelf life ☆☆☆
After a while you will become a master of your seven times table! Once this point is reached you probably won't want to play any more.

The game in more detail
Gather round in a circle. The **go** starts off in a specific direction so the starter **calls**[3] "A game of sevens to my left... one." The go moves on one place and the next player says "Two". The count continues in the same

direction until the seventh go. At this point the player whose go it is must say *anything but* "Seven." After this the go **moves off (M)** in the opposite direction, in this case, right.

This game is really easy. Look at this example game where nobody puts a foot wrong.

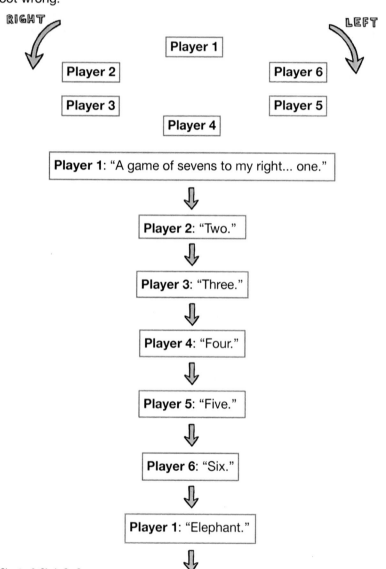

Player 1: "A game of sevens to my right... one."

Player 2: "Two."

Player 3: "Three."

Player 4: "Four."

Player 5: "Five."

Player 6: "Six."

Player 1: "Elephant."

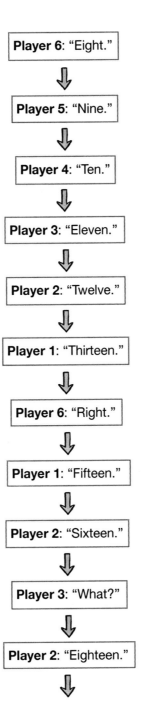

Player 1: "Nineteen."

⬇

Player 6: "Twenty."

⬇

Player 5: "Twenty-plus."

⬇

Player 6: "Twenty-two."

⬇

Player 1: "Twenty-three."

⬇

Player 2: "Twenty-four."

⬇

Player 3: "Twenty-five."

⬇

Player 4: "Twenty-six."

⬇

Player 5: "Sorry?"

⬇

Player 4: "No, after you!"

⬇

Player 5: "Twenty-nine."

INFO+ You're unlikely to get this far if you and your friends are playing for the first time.

As you can see from the example game, if it's your go on a multiple of 7 or a number with 7 in it, you can say what you like as long as it's not the number. You can even say a short sentence although making a speech is **not the done thing (D)!**

One tactic is to pretend not to hear what is said, e.g. "What?" or "Have you had your go?" or "Hold on!"

You could confuse things by saying a number, for example:

Player 6: "Six."

Player 7: "Six."

Player 6: "Eight."

As **Boss** of the game, make sure everyone remembers "**A quick game's a good game (G)!**" If a player hesitates or goes out of turn then they are fined and have to restart the game on "One". The game can restart in any direction, e.g. "A game of sevens to my left… one." This will mix things up even more, making it more difficult. I challenge you to make seventy when you and your friends are drunk — **nigh-on** impossible!

The bottle difference
This is another variation of 'Sevens'. The first difference is you must always say 'bottle' instead of 'seven', multiples of seven or numbers with seven in them. The second difference is that any number that contains numbers which can either be added or subtracted to make seven; should be substituted with 'ding'. For example, sixteen is made from a 1 and a 6 which if added make seven. Also eighteen is made from a 1 and an 8 and if one is subtracted from eight it makes seven.

So I'll show you a quick game of 'Bottle' in the form of a litany of numbers:

One, Two, Three, Four, Five, Six, Bottle, Eight, Nine, Ten, Eleven, Twelve, Thirteen, Bottle, Fifteen, Ding, Bottle, Ding, Nineteen, Twenty, Bottle, Twenty-two, Twenty-three, Twenty-four, Ding, Twenty-six, Bottle… we could go on forever!

The same rules apply as if you were playing 'Sevens' i.e. "bottle" or "ding" reverses the direction of play.

Brief description

Try and count up to twenty-one in sequence, as a group. *Each player can say one, two or three numbers.* One number keeps the **go** going in the direction the game is moving, two numbers reverses the direction of the game and three numbers makes the go skip a player in the direction the game is flowing. The player who reaches twenty-one and says it, has to **down** or **chin** whatever they have for a drink and make up a new rule. This rule usually makes it more difficult to reach twenty-one. The player who reached twenty-one restarts the game.

Number of players

You need at least six players for a good game. Too many people (above twelve say) can be problematic if you are unable to keep everyone's concentration on the game.

Situation

You must be in a reasonably quiet environment so that **calls**[1] can be heard. '21' is regarded as *the* student drinking game and is the game that most people tend to know.

Drinks needed

Any

Difficulty

Medium

INFO+ This is not difficult to learn. You will find it difficult to reach twenty-one after a couple of rules have been implemented.

Intoxication level

Medium

INFO+ It all depends how often you say "Twenty-one".

Implements needed

None

Shelf life ☆☆☆☆

You will definitely return to this game, but it can become so riddled with rules that you may find it impossible to reach twenty-one after playing for some time. When the game becomes too difficult players may lose interest.

The game in more detail
Starting the game

You start by saying "A game of twenty-plus-one to my left," (choosing left *or* right). It is imperative that you do not say "Twenty-one." (I feel bad just writing and thinking it!) Please see the glossary for what can be referred to as **a game of life (G)** syndrome! You *only* say "Twenty-one" in the context of the game if you are forced to. If you want to refer to twenty-one you can say "Three times seven," or "Twenty-plus-one," or "The number before 22." If you say "Twenty-one," by mistake at any time you must drink the rest of your drink. It is then your go to restart from "One." However, if saying "Twenty-one" was the only number you were able to say (i.e. you were forced to say it) you chin your drink but get to make up a rule afterwards. After you have finished making up your rule (see 'Traditional 21 rules' below for examples) and explained it to everyone playing, you then restart the game from "One."

What to do on your go?

You can say one, two or even three sequential numbers *but no more.*

Saying one number carries the go in the direction the game is going.

Saying two numbers reverses the direction of the go.

Saying three numbers makes the go skip a player in the direction it was already going.

No doubling doubles

You can't say a double (i.e. two consecutive numbers) immediately after someone else — you cannot then say a double again as you can't **double a double (D)**. If this does happen then the second 'doubler' is fined and starts the game from "One".

No tripling a triple

You also can't **triple a triple (T)**. For example, if Player 1 says three numbers, the go skips to 7 and Player 7 says three numbers, skipping to Player 5, then 5 cannot say a triple. The player who says the third triple (Player 5 in this example) is fined and has to start the game from "One."

INFO+ The most frequent mistake made is to double a double. If someone sends the go back to you, you'll naturally want to send it straight back to them.

Traditional '21' rules

- no swearing. Any expletives are fined.
- **no pointing (P)** with fingers (you'll be surprised how difficult this is!) Pointing with your elbow is acceptable and will be highly amusing.
- left-hand drinking only (simple but effective.) If anyone drinks with their right hand, **call[4] "Buffalo!"**
- change two numbers in the game around. For example instead of saying "Two", you say "Fifteen" and instead of saying "Fifteen", you say "Two". If we were to count traditionally to provide an example (such a litany of numbers would never happen in '21') "One, fifteen, three, four, five, six, seven, eight, nine, ten, eleven, twelve, thirteen, fourteen, two..."
- also it is traditional in '21' to swap a number for a silly noise, action or another word (often rude). For example:

  "One, two, quack (the player quacks like a duck), four, five..."

  "One, two, three, **cunt**, five..."

  "One two three, (the player stands up and sits down), five..."

Use your imagination and make up the rule to suit the situation. Any rule made can be stopped by the next player to reach twenty-one (usually if it has proved unpopular) or they can add another rule. However, you cannot make a rule to stop a rule *and* make up your own rule. It's either one or the other. As I keep saying "Rules are like wishes, so use them wisely!"

If anyone at any time breaks an established rule they are asked to drink a **finger** and restart the game (much to the consternation of the other players, especially if the game was nearing twenty-one).

A word on starts

On the start you always have to say the direction but you can say one, two or three numbers. If you said "A game of twenty-plus-one to my right...

one, two," the game would move to the player on your left, as two numbers reverses the direction. Likewise if you said "A game of twenty-plus-one to my left… one, two," the game would go to the player on your right. You could also say "A game of twenty-plus-one to my left… one, two, three," and this would mean it is the go of the player two places to your left.

An example game:

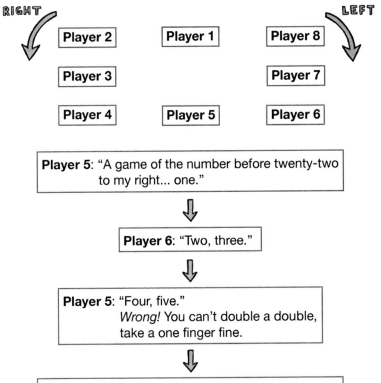

Player 5: "A game of the number before twenty-two to my right… one."

Player 6: "Two, three."

Player 5: "Four, five."
Wrong! You can't double a double, take a one finger fine.

Player 5: "A game of the number before twenty-two to my right… one."

Player 6: "Two."

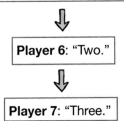

Player 7: "Three."

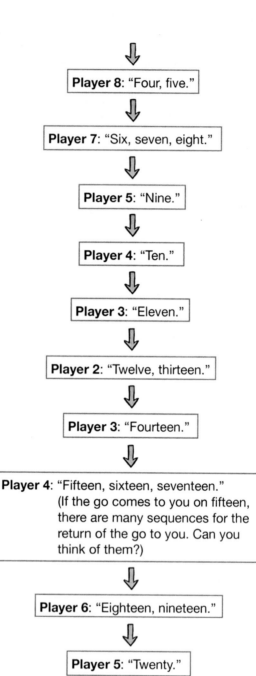

Player 8: "Four, five."

Player 7: "Six, seven, eight."

Player 5: "Nine."

Player 4: "Ten."

Player 3: "Eleven."

Player 2: "Twelve, thirteen."

Player 3: "Fourteen."

Player 4: "Fifteen, sixteen, seventeen."
(If the go comes to you on fifteen, there are many sequences for the return of the go to you. Can you think of them?)

Player 6: "Eighteen, nineteen."

Player 5: "Twenty."

Player 4: "Twenty-one!" *Oops!*
(Fifteen has proved to be **a poisoned chalice (P)**! Player 4 must down their drink and after careful contemplation, decides to swap the number 5 with the number 18.)

Player 4: "A game of the number before twenty-two to my right... one, two."

Player 3: "Three, four, eighteen."

Player 1: "Six, seven."

Player 2: "Eight."

Player 2: "Nine, ten, eleven."

Player 3: "Twelve, thirteen, fourteen."

Player 5: "Fifteen."

Player 8: "Sixteen."

Player 1: "Seventeen, five, nineteen."

Player 3: "Twenty."

Player 4: "Twenty-one!" *Oops!*
(They down their drink and say "The number 10 will be changed to an action or sound of celebration!")

Player 4: "A game of three times seven to my right... one, two, three."

Player 6: "Four, eighteen, six."

Player 8: "Seven, eight."

Player 7: "Nine."

Player 6: "Yes! Get in!"

Player 5: "Eleven, twelve."

Player 6: "Thirteen, fourteen, fifteen."

Player 8: "Sixteen."

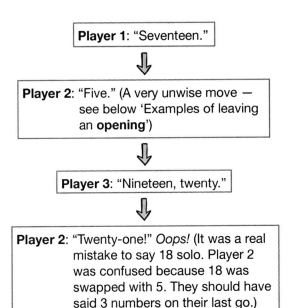

Player 1: "Seventeen."

Player 2: "Five." (A very unwise move — see below 'Examples of leaving an **opening**')

Player 3: "Nineteen, twenty."

Player 2: "Twenty-one!" *Oops!* (It was a real mistake to say 18 solo. Player 2 was confused because 18 was swapped with 5. They should have said 3 numbers on their last go.)

INFO+ A game of '21' stops when it is agreed everyone has had enough. Once too many rules are instituted you will find that the frequency of making twenty-one drops. When it has become almost impossible to make twenty-one because there is a minefield of rules to negotiate, then the game is likely to become frustrating.

You can play the game '21' without reading any further notes (below). However, you may like to read the notes on **check outs (C¹)** (the skill by which you avoid saying "twenty-one" if possible) and on leaving openings, i.e. what you don't want to do!

Further notes for veterans

A check out in '21' is being able to say a number nearing twenty-one in the knowledge that the go won't return to you and force you to say "twenty-one". The simplest check out is if the go comes to you on "nineteen" you say "twenty". By saying "twenty" it is impossible for anyone to make you say "twenty-one" because the player after you will have to say it.

Openings

Let us look at an example that is not a check out. The go comes to you on "seventeen" and you stupidly say just "eighteen." You have left yourself exposed. Now the player next to you could say "Nineteen, twenty," sending the go back to you and forcing you to say "twenty-one". If you foolishly backed yourself into such an avoidable "twenty-one", it is said that you've left an opening.

INFO+ When the game is nearing sixteen start thinking "How am I going to avoid getting the go back and having to utter the **unmentionable word (U)**?"

An example of a **classy** check out[2]:

We'll pick the game up at 16 going left...

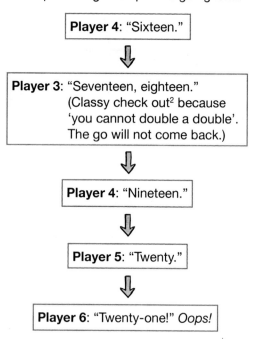

Player 4: "Sixteen."

⇩

Player 3: "Seventeen, eighteen."
(Classy check out[2] because
'you cannot double a double'.
The go will not come back.)

⇩

Player 4: "Nineteen."

⇩

Player 5: "Twenty."

⇩

Player 6: "Twenty-one!" *Oops!*

Examples of leaving an opening:

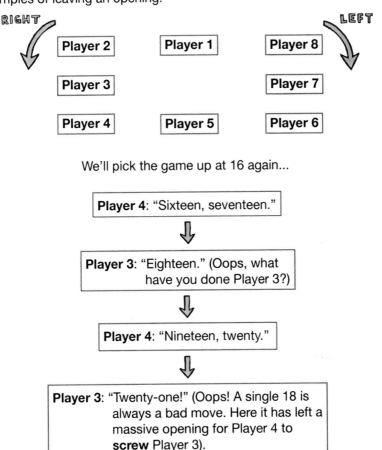

We'll pick the game up at 16 again...

> **Player 4**: "Sixteen, seventeen."

⬇

> **Player 3**: "Eighteen." (Oops, what have you done Player 3?)

⬇

> **Player 4**: "Nineteen, twenty."

⬇

> **Player 3**: "Twenty-one!" (Oops! A single 18 is always a bad move. Here it has left a massive opening for Player 4 to **screw** Player 3).

Please never leave an opening like that!

Variation: Ali G Roman numeral 21

(a.k.a. the elite version of '21')

Brief description
This is exactly the same game as '21' but we use **Roman numerals (R)**.
Look through the example of Roman numerals '21' below before I **drop the bomb (B)** of **Ali G's (A)** involvement!

Number of players
It's unlikely that you know many people who will be able to play this version of '21'. I'd say four or five players is perfect, as any more will just confuse things, whilst less will mean skip-a-gos don't work as they should.

Situation
You are with elite drinkers, **veterans** of '21'. Some of you might have had grounding in basic Latin numeracy (though I never did so don't worry, if you haven't, you'll learn!)

Drinks needed
Any

Difficulty
Complex

Intoxication level
Medium

Implements needed
Nothing except a brain, which could outwit **Stephen Fry (F)**.

The game in more detail
Understand '21' before you attempt this!

An example of Roman numeral '21':

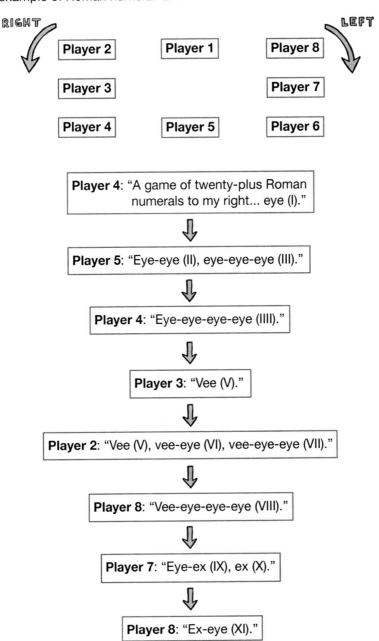

RIGHT

LEFT

Player 2	Player 1	Player 8
Player 3		Player 7
Player 4	Player 5	Player 6

Player 4: "A game of twenty-plus Roman numerals to my right... eye (I)."

⬇

Player 5: "Eye-eye (II), eye-eye-eye (III)."

⬇

Player 4: "Eye-eye-eye-eye (IIII)."

⬇

Player 3: "Vee (V)."

⬇

Player 2: "Vee (V), vee-eye (VI), vee-eye-eye (VII)."

⬇

Player 8: "Vee-eye-eye-eye (VIII)."

⬇

Player 7: "Eye-ex (IX), ex (X)."

⬇

Player 8: "Ex-eye (XI)."

Player 1: "Ex-eye-eye (XII), ex-eye-eye-eye (XIII), ex-eye-vee (XIV)."

Player 3: "Ex-vee (XV)."

Player 4: "Ex-vee-eye (XVI), ex-vee-eye-eye (XVII)."

Player 3: "Ex-vee-eye-eye-eye (XVIII)." (A silly move Player 3. You said 18 solo. You've left an **opening** to get punished, you really need to pay more attention!)

Player 2: "Ex-eye-ex (XIX), ex-ex (XX)."

Player 3: "Ex-ex-eye (XXI)." (That's 21! Now Player 3 makes up a rule after drinking their drink **in one (O)**.)

OK! Who the **fuck**[1] thinks of these games?!

Right, now you'll play Roman numeral '21' in the style of Ali G, prepare yourself! All the rules are of course exactly the same as '21' but the way you *say* the number is different.

I = put an Ali G accent on "eye"
V = "**Me Julie (J)**"
X = "**Hear me now (H)**"

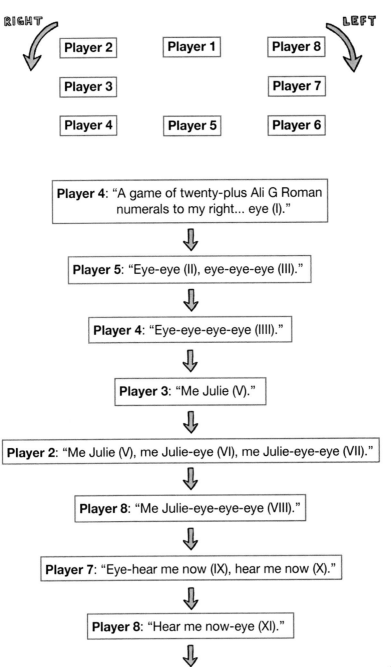

RIGHT

LEFT

Player 2   Player 1   Player 8

Player 3   Player 7

Player 4   Player 5   Player 6

Player 4: "A game of twenty-plus Ali G Roman numerals to my right... eye (I)."

Player 5: "Eye-eye (II), eye-eye-eye (III)."

Player 4: "Eye-eye-eye-eye (IIII)."

Player 3: "Me Julie (V)."

Player 2: "Me Julie (V), me Julie-eye (VI), me Julie-eye-eye (VII)."

Player 8: "Me Julie-eye-eye-eye (VIII)."

Player 7: "Eye-hear me now (IX), hear me now (X)."

Player 8: "Hear me now-eye (XI)."

Player 7: "Hear me now-eye-eye (XII), hear me now-eye -eye-eye (XIII), hear me now-eye-me Julie (XIV)."

Player 5: "Hear me now-me Julie (XV)."

Player 4: "Hear me now-me Julie-eye (XVI), hear me now-me Julie-eye-eye (XVII)."

Player 5: "Hear me now-me Julie-eye-eye-eye (XVIII)." (A silly move, this is an 18!)

Player 6: "Hear me now-eye-hear me now (XIX), hear me now-hear me now (XX)."

Player 5: "Hear me now-hear me now-eye (XXI)." (21!)

It will be a miracle if you ever make XXI ('21'), let alone adding rules to make it harder! Enjoy, you psychos!

Gloucester Directions

Brief description

Use the **calls**[1] 'left' and 'right' to pass the **go** round the circle. 'Left' sends the go to the right and 'right' sends the go to the left. Add in the call[1] "Wheressatto?" (where's that to?) to send the go to the player with whom you make eye contact.

I come from Bristol so this game makes sense to me in the form below. Learn the principle and change the name and calls[1] to suit your **geo-socio situation (G)**.

Number of players

More than four players is a good idea.

Situation

You need to hear what people are saying, so a reasonably quiet atmosphere.

Drinks needed

Any

Difficulty

Hard

INFO+ This quickly gets confusing.

Intoxication level

Medium

Implements needed

None

Shelf life ☆☆☆

Very soon your brain will adjust to 'right' being left and 'left' being right. When this happens you'll find you will need to stop playing as the game will become too easy.

The game in more detail
This game is based on the mixing up of right and left so that a call[1] of 'left' means the game moves right and a call[1] of 'right' means the game moves left. In 'Gloucester Directions' therefore (as in real life when you are given directions in Gloucester) the opposite of the direction given is always true.

Starting the game
To start this game, all participants must be in a rough circle, e.g. sitting round a table. To start the game you say:

"A game of Gloucester Directions, to my…"

Next you say *the actual direction* you intend the game to proceed in, followed immediately by the 'Gloucester Directions' call[1] which sends the go that way. For instance, if you want the game to go right in real terms you would say "A game of Gloucester Directions to my right... left."

Follow-on calls
The next call[1] must be made by the player to the right of the starter. Follow-on calls[1] are either 'left' or 'right'. So let's say, for example, the player to the right says "left" then the game will continue right passing to the next player to the right. If this player then says "right", the game goes back to the left.

Here's a quick demonstration to illustrate the basics:

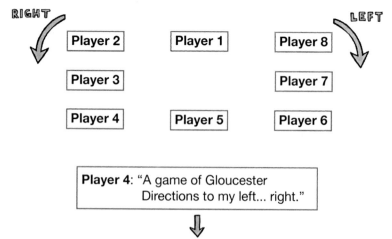

RIGHT

LEFT

| Player 2 | Player 1 | Player 8 |

| Player 3 | | Player 7 |

| Player 4 | Player 5 | Player 6 |

Player 4: "A game of Gloucester Directions to my left... right."

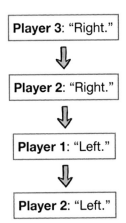

| Player 3: "Right." |
| Player 2: "Right." |
| Player 1: "Left." |
| Player 2: "Left." |

After you have mastered the basics, add the "Where's that to?" call[1].

Say: "Where's that to?" in a Gloucester accent — "wheressatto?", much like a farmer.

What does it do and what do you do? If you have the go, you look directly at any other player and say "Where's that to?" (like a 'Zoom' in 'Zoom, Schwartz, Pafigliano' (see p71) or a 'Pong' in 'Ping-Pang-Pong' (see p64)).

Player 8 asks Player 5 "Wheresattoo?" and makes eye contact. It will be Player 5's go next.

The **power**, i.e. the go, is now with the player who has been 'looked at' and they can decide to say 'left' or 'right' or look at another player and say "Where's that to?". They must not "Where's that to?" at the player who looked at them. This is a misdemeanour and must be punished.

Fines
Common mistakes, which are to be fined are:
- hesitation
- calling[1] when it is not your go
- saying "Where's that to?" to a player who has just asked you that question.

Using your eyes
As in many **circle go games (C)**, using your eyes is a good way to get your fellow players confused. If you say "Right," look convincingly at the person to your right, even though the game goes to the left. It's surprising how many people will be fooled by this simple trick. If this is picked up, then you might try a **double bluff (B)** and if you say "Left," look right convincingly.

This game is all about who has the strength of mind to cope with the confusion!

A word on restarts
Unlike other circle go games, if someone **messes up (M)** (of course they must be fined) they must restart the game, as it's difficult to get the start right due to its confusing nature. They might end up drinking again and there is nothing more entertaining than a **repeat offender (R)**!

Now I'll show an example of a game with the "Where's that to?" rule with mess ups included:

Player 2: "A game of 'Gloucester Directions' to my right... left."

⬇

Player 3: "Left."

⬇

Player 4: "Left."

⬇

Player 5: "Wheresattoo?"
(looks at Player 8)

⬇

Player 8: "Wheresattoo?"
(looks at Player 1)

⬇

Player 1: "Right."

⬇

Player 8: "Right."

⬇

Player 7: "Wheresattoo?"
(looks at Player 2)

⬇

Player 2: "Wheresattoo?"
(looks at Player 7)
Wrong! Player 2 drinks and restarts the game.

⬇

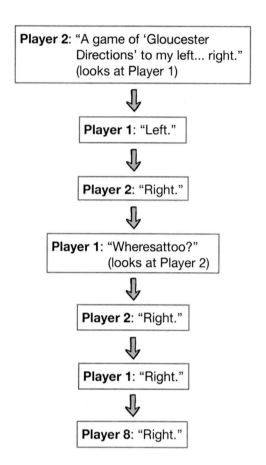

Player 2: "A game of 'Gloucester Directions' to my left... right." (looks at Player 1)

⬇

Player 1: "Left."

⬇

Player 2: "Right."

⬇

Player 1: "Wheresattoo?" (looks at Player 2)

⬇

Player 2: "Right."

⬇

Player 1: "Right."

⬇

Player 8: "Right."

Hope you've not got lost?

New rules

Be inventive and creative with this game. If you get bored of the "Where's that to?" rule, try inventing your own.

e.g. Player 1 sends the go to Player 8 with a call of "Right." Player 8 calls "Flyover!"

This new call could make the power skip a go to the left so it passes to Player 6. Adding local accents makes the game more entertaining. You may have realised that I'm a **West Country (W)** Boy, but modify the game to a town or city near you.

Chapter 4
Group Games

 ## Slammers, Sliders, Spiders

Brief description
Break into two teams with an equal number of players on each side. This game is similar to 'Team Spoof' (p21). However, in this game, the idea is to work out which player is concealing a single coin. The coin must be presented with one of three pre-set hand actions – slammers, sliders or spiders.

Number of players
Six, eight or ten players. Any more and it would get quite crowded.

Situation
A bar, pub or **pre-lash (P)**. This game needs to be played in a reasonably quiet atmosphere so that players can listen for the sound of a coin hitting the table.

Drinks needed
Anything you're drinking.

Difficulty
Medium
INFO+ Not difficult to learn but can be difficult to play. Hand dexterity is the key.

Intoxication level
Medium

Implements needed
One large coin (usually a 10p) and a table (preferably long and thin).

Playing either side of a bar is ideal, with one team on the customers' side and the other on the bartender's side.

Shelf life ☆☆☆☆☆

A great (G)! Get a bit of competition going and the hours will fly by! This looks so cool you'll come back to it again and again.

The game in more detail

First of all decide which team will have the coin first. It's probably best to flip the coin for this. The team that wins the flip and takes the coin is the action team a.k.a. the presenting team. The team without the coin (the team that lost the flip) is the non-action side, a.k.a. the **calling**[2] team. It is best to sit on opposite sides of a narrow table. You are now sitting facing your opponents at very close quarters.

The presenting team and the calling team ready to play

On the presenting side, the coin must be secretly distributed to a member of the team (do this under the table) before the **round**[2] of play commences. There is no verbal discussion about which team member gets the coin. Whoever wants it (if you're feeling confident of your skills, you're likely to want the coin) takes it in the hand-off under the table.

The presenting team (i.e. the team with the coin in play) then presents one closed fist per player. They keep the other hand closed behind their backs.

Waiting to perform the 'Show'. The calling team will say 'Slammers', 'Sliders' or 'Spiders'

The action call and the 'Show'

The calling[2] team call "Slammers", "Sliders" or "Spiders". The 'action call[1]' dictates what action the other team must perform (see below). The goal of the presenting team is to disguise which player has the coin whilst doing the action selected by the calling[2] team.

The presenting team now performs the 'Show' in their own time. It's best for the presenting team to count themselves into performing the 'Show,' i.e. "1, 2, 3, show." This helps hide the sound of the coin on a 'Slammer' or a 'Slider', and gives multiple targets to analyse on a 'Spider'. The calling[2] team cannot make the same call[1] twice in a row. They must make a different call each time.

The actions

1. Slammer

A 'Slammer' is simply banging your hand down with an open palm. Do this quickly enough, and together, and the other team will have trouble locating the coin. See photo on next page.

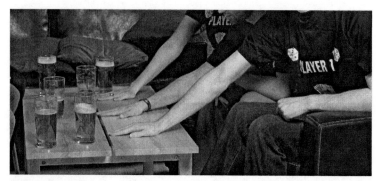
Slammer

2. Slider

A 'Slider' is like a 'Slammer' but once you have your hand down, you pull it back a couple of inches. This helps the calling team, locate the coin as after the bang of the slam you can hear the scrape of the coin in the slide.

3. Spider

To make a 'Spider', the idea is to squeeze the coin into the palm of the hand, and on the 'Show', put your finger tips on the table, splayed out to look like a spider. Everyone's 'Spider' looks different and you may find that some players cannot make a 'Spider', especially if they have small hands. On the 'Spider' call[1] it is as much about the rest of the presenting team creating convincing fake 'Spiders', as it is about the player with the coin making a good 'Spider'. The 'Spider' is the only action in which the coin doesn't hit the table.

Presenting 'Spiders' in the 'Show'

Call[2] and reveal

The calling[2] team will now select which hand they think holds the coin. Choosing which hand to **call**[3] is a group decision by the calling[2] team. This may provoke lively discussions as players will not always agree. Once the calling[2] team has made their call the presenting team must reveal who on their team really has the coin. This reveal can take the form of elimination to add suspense.

The calling[2] team chooses one player at a time from the presenting team who they think does not have the coin. They say, "You haven't got the coin Player X so take away your hand." The calling[2] team wins if they manage to keep eliminating players from the presenting team until only the player with the coin is left. If this happens the presenting team is fined.

But if the calling[2] team guesses wrong, and tells a player who does have the coin to remove their hand from the table, that player reveals the coin to the calling[2] team. The presenting team has won and the calling team is fined.

If the calling[2] team has selected incorrectly, then each player on this team is fined and the game continues with them making a new action call[3] for the presenting team. Remember this cannot be the same action call[3] as the one they have just made.

If the calling[2] team selects correctly, then each player on the presenting team is fined and the coin is handed from the presenting team to the calling[2] team.

The roles are now reversed and the presenting team becomes the calling[2] team and vice versa. A good level of fining is needed to create tension and put pressure on the actions made by the presenting team, and the call[3] made by the calling[2] team.

This game looks cool, it trains the dexterity of your hands and perfects the art of **bluff**. Enjoy!

 # Titanic

Brief description
A glass floats (open end up) in a jug of beer. On your **go**, pour as much or as little of your own drink as you like into the glass which will make it float lower in the jug. Whoever makes the glass completely sink on their go, will have to pull the glass out of the jug and **down** the contents.

Number of players
At least two players but no more than ten because if numbers are too high, not everyone will have a go before the 'boat' sinks.

Situation
This often involves a lot of mess and could be described as a 'water sport'. The ideal situation is outside on a summer's day either at an understanding pub or at a garden party.

Drinks needed
Lots and lots of **beer** or cider.

Difficulty
Easy
INFO+ Not difficult to play but difficult to keep a steady hand under pressure.

Intoxication level
High

Implements needed
A large jug that holds at least 1.5 pints and a pint glass or a half pint glass which will float in a stable fashion in this jug of liquid. It's a good idea to practice floating the glass in a jug of water to ensure that you don't spill valuable alcohol. Any glass that is too heavy will sink as soon as it is placed in the jug. A glass that is too buoyant will not stay upright.

Shelf life ☆☆☆

I love this game because of the spectacle it creates and the excitement and anticipation a vessel creates when it is teetering on the brink of sinking. However this game can lose its fun after too many **rounds**[2].

The game in more detail

Before starting this game think about the people with whom you are playing. Will every player be able to drink a pint **in one (O)**? If not, you should play with a smaller glass. Also have plenty of beer or cider on hand to keep the jug topped up.

The pint glass is weighted with alcohol, ready for the game to start

Fill the jug almost to the top, but leave enough space to allow the glass to sink without the contents of the jug spilling out. To start the game, float the glass on top of the jug full of drink. You may need to weigh the glass down with a small amount of drink to make it float steadily before you start. The idea is to pour as much or as little of your own drink as you like into the floating glass when it is your turn. Players take it in turn to add drink and the go moves round the group in the same direction throughout the game. The glass will sink lower into the jug each time more is added. There will come a point when the weight of the glass will become too much for the surface tension and the glass will sink rapidly to the bottom of the jug as liquid rushes in over the sides.

On your go, add contributions to the glass as shown here, and not the jug

The person who sinks the drink must pull the full glass out and drink the contents in one — "Whoever sinks it, drinks it!"

Glass on the brink of sinking

Sometimes the glass takes a while to sink as tiny amounts of liquid trickle over the lip from the jug, so allow each player a couple of seconds' grace before they add more drink to the glass. If the glass sinks during the grace period the previous player downs the contents of the glass. If it doesn't sink the game continues.

Any **underhanded** antics like hitting the table when the glass is teetering on the brink are not allowed. If any player is employing such tactics, I suggest that they should be fined by having to pull the glass out and drink the contents. After all, you reap what you sow! After a fine is taken make sure the jug is topped up to replace the lost liquid. The game restarts with the empty glass being returned to the jug with a little liquid in it for stability. After this the go passes to the player one place on from the player who **fucked-up**[3].

I Have Never...

Brief description
The first player says something that he or she has never done, e.g. "I have never been to Glasgow." All those who have been to Glasgow will have to own up and drink a one **finger** fine. You're not allowed to lie, e.g. to say, "I have never been to Amsterdam," if you've actually been as you will be fined (although it's sometimes worth the punishment to expose someone else who you know has done something embarrassing!)

Number of players
More than three players. The larger the group the better.

Situation
A little 'get to know each other'! You'll need to play this with at least a couple of players who know one another very well because they'll have plenty of **ammo** on their so-called 'friends'. You must be able to hear what each player is saying, so nowhere too loud.

Drinks needed
Anything you're drinking.

Difficulty
Easy

Intoxication level
Medium
INFO+ If you have a **chequered past (C)** you could be drinking quite a bit! Intoxication level will be high if you're a bad boy or girl!

Implements needed
None

Shelf life ☆☆☆
This game is **a great (G)** and you'll return to it again and again with different friends. Nevertheless, the game does lose its excitement once

everything is **outed**[3,] (i.e. all the worst secrets have been revealed).

The game in more detail

You will uncover your friends' darkest secrets during this game. It can be most enjoyable to **stitch up (S)** one of your friends, by exposing something horrendous which you know they have said or done.

You start the game by saying "I have never…" (plus something you have *not done* but you suspect someone else might have). You will find that 'I Have Never…' soon starts to focus around sex and/or embarrassing situations.

Anyone who has done the thing you suggest will drink a fine (usually one **finger**). They must be honest! Obviously it's up to the player who has done the thing mentioned to be honest and drink but if a number of players know it to be true, then they might add some pressure by saying:

"Are you sure you haven't done that Player X?"

If you say "I have never…" and it turns out that no one has done it, then you must drink for making such a poor **call**[2].

The **go** moves round the players in order and the direction of play must not be changed.

Be warned — introduce a game of 'I Have Never…' at your peril!

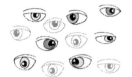 # Paranoia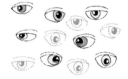

Brief description
Option 1: Whisper a secret or harmless fact about one of the group to the player on your left or right and they then point at the player the secret or fact concerns.

Option 2: On your **go** you whisper a question to the player on your left or right, e.g. "In your view, who's the ugliest person here?". They then answer the question by pointing at another player.

With both options, if the player being pointed at wants to know what has been said about them they must finish their drink.

Number of players
Four players or more.

Situation
Gather a group of friends. It is best to have at least a couple of people who have known each other for a little while. Unlike 'I Have Never...' (see p112), you can play this in a noisy environment because you will be whispering into the ear of the player next to you.

Drinks needed
Any

Difficulty
Easy
INFO+ It could be a painfully embarrassing night.

Intoxication level
High
INFO+ Although this depends on your level of paranoia.

Implements needed
None

Shelf life ☆☆☆

Unfortunately once everyone knows everyone else's darkest secrets then there will no more **ammo** to play with.

What's being said about you?

The game in more detail

This game is simple but a lot of fun. It's like a whispered version of 'I Have Never…' (see p112) with the option of remaining unaware of what has been said about you.

Option 1

First decide whether the go is going to pass to the left or the right. You then tell the next player a secret or a harmless fact and point at the person it concerns, e.g:

"Here's a good one. Did you know that Rob has…!"

"Listen up, I saw Kate… yesterday!"

"Right **get**[3] this! Sam and Alice were… last night!"

Or you could **bluff** with an innocent fact:

"Beth is 20 years old."

"Jack is taller than I am."

Option 2

Play moves round the circle as in Option 1. Start by asking the person next to you a question and then tell them to point at the player who in their view answers the question, e.g:

"Who do you think has...?"

"Who is the... here?"

"Who would you most like to... with?"

These can be quite embarrassing for both the player pointed at and the player who is pointing.

In both cases (however harmless or reputation destroying) the player pointing must give an honest answer!

With both options, if the player who is pointed at is 'paranoid' wants to know what has been said about them, then they must drink all of their drink. This can be either down **in one (O)** or you may allow players to finish all their drink in more than one attempt as long as they don't dawdle (this detail needs to be decided before play commences). When the drink is finished the person who answered the question must reveal what has been said to the group. The person who is pointed at can also choose silence, i.e. proving that they don't want or need to know. In this case they *do not* need to drink their drink and are 'not paranoid'.

It is now the turn of the player who pointed in the last go to ask a question. The new question can target any player, even the one who was pointed at on the last go.

This game can **out**[3] a lot of players' secrets! It is also highly amusing if someone drinks their drink in paranoia, only to find out that the 'secret' was a completely innocuous fact like "Steve wears glasses," or "Kerry drives." It wasn't what they feared coming out[3], e.g. "Steve loves dressing up in his mother's clothes," or "Kerry works as a stripper!"

A really great group bonding game!

Bunnies

a.k.a Moose, Stags, Aliens or Captain Bigglesworth

Brief description

If you have the **go**, i.e. the **power**, you perform a specific action. Those to your immediate left and right perform set actions in response to yours. You can keep the power for as long as you like, so long as you keep performing the action. You then pass it to another player in the group. Confused already? Read below and **check out (C²)** the images.

Number of players

More than six players is recommended for 'Bunnies' and 'Aliens'. For 'Captain **Biggles**worth' you need at least seven players but I propose you play with ten or more.

Situation

All versions of this game are very silly so you will probably need to be quite **merry** to play them. As this game is played with actions, once you know it you can play in even the loudest of places.

Drinks needed

Any

Difficulty

Medium

INFO+ 'Bunnies' and 'Aliens' are very easy to learn but 'Captain Bigglesworth' is somewhat harder.

Intoxication level

Low

INFO+ This is not a **lash** game.

Implements needed

None

Shelf life ☆☆☆

'Bunnies' and 'Aliens' will last you quite a few **rounds²** before you tire of them. 'Captain Bigglesworth' (due to its hilarity and complexity) will last longer.

The game in more detail

There are three variations which I'll explain here. The first two games, 'Bunnies' and 'Aliens' are the basic versions and involve no more than three players at any one time performing actions. 'Captain Bigglesworth' is more difficult and requires several people to perform the actions. All these games can be changed to suit your own style or **banter** once you understand the concept.

'Bunnies' in detail — the most widely known variation of this game
The person with the go puts both hands over their head like bunny ears.

The Bunny/the go/the power

The player to the right is half a bunny and puts their left hand over their head as a bunny ear. The player to the left is also half a bunny and puts their right hand on their head as a bunny ear. So three players are doing actions! A whole bunny at the centre and two half bunnies either side.

'Bunnies' set up with the go on Player 4

If the player with the power, i.e. 'the bunny', wants to pass the go on, they must take their hands off their head and point them both in the direction of another player.

Throwing the go

This player can be anywhere in the group and even one of the players to the left or right who was previously a half bunny. You are not allowed to pass a bunny back to the player who passed to you.

You can also make a dummy, or fake, **call**[1]. To do this you point with your fingertips but *do not* let your thumbs leave your face or head.

Dummy throwing the go

Fines

Players are fined if they react to dummy calls[1]. They are also fined if they fail to react and accept the go being passed onto them. The players to the left and right of anyone receiving the go are also expected to react. If they do not, they are also fined. Putting the wrong hand up to make a half bunny is a common mistake.

A common mistake. Player 12 on the right has the wrong ear!

I'll now show you an example game and what actions are expected.

Player 1 has the go. Players to the left and right here reacting correctly

What happens next?
Player 1 throws the go to Player 3.

The go is with Player 3

Player 2 has gone from being a left-handed half bunny to a right-handed bunny on the left of the player with the go.

What happens next?
Now Player 3 passes the go to Player 4.

Player 4 has gone from being a left-handed bunny to being the go

Player 4 was previously a left-handed bunny, to the right of the go and is now 'the bunny'.

'Aliens' in detail
This is a more masculine variation of 'Bunnies'. I think that playing 'Bunnies', especially with a big group of lads, can look a bit **gay**! So I play variations **called**[7] 'Aliens' and 'Moose'. In 'Moose' you substitute stag antlers for the bunny ears. In 'Aliens' you pass the 'alien disease'.

The Alien disease action: The alien, i.e. the person with the go, frantically pretends to wash their face without touching it. Try it and you'll see what I mean! Imagine you've got a virile alien disease on your face.

The Alien disease!

What are the players to the right and the left doing?
The player to the right uses their left hand to pretend to frantically scrub the left side of their face. The player to the left uses their right hand to pretend to frantically scrub the right side of their face.

Player 4 with the alien/the go

See the next page for how to play the Captain Bigglesworth variation.

Captain Bigglesworth

An elite variation of 'Bunnies'. Prepare yourself, you are in for a treat! This is quite possibly the silliest game in the whole of *The Lash*.

Making 'Captain Bigglesworth'
The player who has the **go** is called[7] Captain Bigglesworth a.k.a Biggles. They are distinguished by their flight goggles. These are made by placing the thumb and forefinger of both hands together to make a circle. After this invert your hands so that your palms are on your face with your wrists above your eyes and your fingers touch your ears and neck. This is not the most comfortable way to hold your hands and you'll look very silly as you strain to keep your goggles on.

The go, a.k.a. Biggles

Just imagine you are travelling at speed through the air with goggles on!

Making the flying machines
The game operates *on exactly the same principle* as 'Bunnies' and 'Aliens' except the actions can extend much further from the go. Players up to three places to the left or right in the circle can be forced into action to form flying machines. Moving the go can be faked as in 'Aliens' and 'Bunnies'. As

you move the go on, by pointing as explained in 'Bunnies', you must also shout the name of the flying machine which the new Biggles will control. If Captain Bigglesworth passes the go and **calls**[1] out "Glider!", a glider is formed by the new Biggles and the players to either side.

If he or she calls[1] "Chinook!" the new players form a helicopter. See below for the actions.

If no machine is shouted by the player passing the go then the previous flying machine is still in play.

The flying machines
Glider
The simplest flying machine. In the Glider the person to the left of the Captain has the left arm outstretched at shoulder height as a wing. The person to the right, likewise has their right arm out as the right wing.

Position	To go's right	Centre (the go)	To go's left
Part in machine	Right wing	Capt. Bigglesworth	Left wing
Action	Right arm out	Goggles on	Left arm out

Glider

Chinook

Position	To go's right	Centre (the go)	To go's left
Part in machine	Right rotor blade	Capt. Bigglesworth	Left rotor blade
Action	Left arm in air lasso (INFO+)*	Goggles on	Right arm in air lasso (INFO+)*

INFO+ Notice that on a Chinook, the players to the left and right use their inside and not their outside arms as rotor blades.

Chinook

Biplane a.k.a The Sopwith Camel (S)
Biggles' favourite in WWI.

Position	Far right	To go's right	Centre (the go)	To go's left	Far left
Part in machine	Right wing	Engine	Capt. Biggles-worth	Engine	Left wing
Action	Both arms to the right as a wing	Hands rounded	Goggles on	Hands rounded	Both arms to the left as a wing

Biplane

Making an engine action

Round your arms as though you are rocking a baby at waist height. This is the pretend engine turbine. Shake as if you've a chronic case of **Parkinson's Disease (P)** and make the "brrrrrrrrrrrrhhhhh" noise of a **Lancaster Bomber (L)**.

Brrrrrrrrrrrrrhhhhh!

Making a biplane wing

To make a **biplane** wing put both arms out straight to the left or right as though you're clasping a large box at shoulder height. See next page.

A biplane wing

INFO+ If you know your history, you will know that actually a biplane only has one engine but for the sake of symmetry, you're going to have to pretend there are two engines, one on each wing.

Jet

Position	Far right	To go's right	Centre (the go)	To go's left	Far left
Part in machine	Right wing	Engine	Capt. Bigglesworth	Engine	Left wing
Action	Right arm as a wing	Hands rounded	Goggles on	Hands rounded	Left arm as a wing

Making a jet engine

Round and shake your arms just as you did for the biplane engine. This time make the noise of an **F-14 Tomcat (F)** at the start of *Top Gun* **(T)**, i.e. a loud "wrrrrrrrrrrrrrhhhhhhhhhh!" noise.

INFO+ The Jet wing is similar to the Glider wing. You could bend your arms back to make it look more convincing.

Fighter Jet ready for action

Jumbo

Position	Far right	Middle right	To go's right	Centre (the go)	To go's left	Middle left	Far left
Part in machine	Right wing	Engine	Engine	Capt. Biggles-worth	Engine	Engine	Left wing
Action	Right arm as a wing	Round hands	Round hands	Goggles on	Round hands	Round hands	Left arm as a wing

INFO+ The noise created by the **Jumbo** should be deafening!

The creation of the Jumbo

This is the king of aircraft. I'm sure you will be thinking 'What the **fuck**[1] am I doing?' as you form this Biggles machine with your friends. However, you'll be surprised at the sense of achievement!

Animal Kingdom
a.k.a Noah's ark

Brief description

Perform the action for your animal, then another player's animal, to pass the **go** to another player in the circle. If you make a mistake you'll move to the bottom of the group, i.e. 'The Kingdom' and everyone else moves up an animal.

Number of players

Six players or more for a good game.

Situation

This game will attract attention to your group. If this isn't a problem then once the very easy principle of this game is mastered it can be played anywhere. It can be played in silence so it's a good game to play in a place where a rowdy game might be **frowned upon (F)**. You'll probably need to be **half cut (H)** to start this game as it's very silly.

Drinks needed

Just whatever you have in your hand at the time of playing.

Difficulty

Easy

Intoxication level

Low

Implements needed

None

Shelf life ☆☆☆

Creating new animals will keep the interest in this game alive. Competing to getting to the top of the 'Animal Kingdom' will ensure this game remains fun.

The game in more detail

'Animal Kingdom' always starts with the **amoeba** and ends with the lion, respectively the lowest creature and 'the king' of the animal world. The animals which you choose between the amoeba and the lion are up to you but they must come in order of status. Status is usually denoted by size and a general rule is that a predator is higher than its prey but it's up to you to decide what relative significance to attribute to each animal. Each animal needs a sign, e.g. a rabbit could be 'bunny ears'. Deciding as a group on the animals to use and the actions for each one is part of the fun of the game. Don't pick animals that would have similar iconic signs, e.g. a fox and a cat in the same game would not be a smart move.

	Creature	Sign	
Player 1	Amoeba	Make a rectangle with thumb and finger of each hand	
Player 2	Worm	Place palms together and 'snake' your hands up	
Player 3	Hedgehog	Put hands together on the back of your head like spikes	
Player 4	Dog	Tongue out and hands like paws begging	
Player 5	Horse	Play the rider by holding the reins and move your body like you're trotting	
Player 6	Gorilla	Fists beat chest	
Player 7	Elephant	Swinging arm as a trunk in front of the nose	
Player 8	Lion	Arms up and fingers spread as claws	

Starting a game

A game is always started by the amoeba. The amoeba makes their sign and then makes the sign of the animal they want the go to pass to. This player then makes their own sign, followed by that of any other player around the table *except the amoeba*. You're not allowed to pass the go to the player who just passed it to you.

Octopus — hands and arms move like tentacles

Let's look at a quick example of a game with the eight animals listed above.

Player 1: Amoeba, lion. The go passes to…

Player 8: Lion, elephant. The go passes to…

Player 7: Elephant…You should **get**[1] the picture!

Fines

I recommend a couple of **fingers** of drink if you:
- are too slow making your sign
- make the wrong sign
- make a confused sign
- send the go back to the person who just sent it to you.

Starting again

The offending player has to move to the bottom of the 'Animal Kingdom', taking on the role of the amoeba and everyone else moves up one animal. This is where it gets exciting as you are now a new animal ("What am I now?" you ask yourself). There must be no **coaching**[2], i.e. helping a fellow player. Any coaching must be crushed with an **iron fist (I)**. Fine any **coachers**[1] heavily! The game will only last as long as changing animals is difficult. If you allow players to remind each other what animal they have now become, they will find the game too easy.

INFO+ You can also add noises for the animals if you want, although personally I prefer this game without.

Fag Game

Brief description
A small coin, such as a 5p or 1p, is suspended above an empty pint glass using toilet paper. Players then take it in turns to burn holes in the paper until the coin drops. The player who makes the coin drop is fined.

Number of players
You can play with two players or more. I believe four is an ideal number, more than six is too many.

Situation
Obviously, a venue where smoking *is* permitted. When playing outside, I've found that many bars and pubs might still give you the old **health and safety (H) chat**[2] if they don't want you playing this game.

Drinks needed
Anything

Difficulty
Easy
INFO+ Get the game set up and it's easy to play.

Intoxication level
Low
INFO+ If you drop the coin more than once this rating will be significantly higher.

Implements needed
A pint glass, some toilet paper and some cigarettes (**straights** work better than **roll ups (R)**).

Shelf life ☆☆☆
This is **a great (G)** game, but restricted as to where you can play it.

Set up and ready to play

Burning a cigarette ends diameter

The coin is still suspended!

The game in more detail
Set up

You require an empty pint glass. You then need one sheet of toilet paper, which should be large enough to cover the open end of the pint glass. Lick your finger and use your saliva (or alternatively you can just use water or some drink) to seal the paper to the rim of the glass all the way round. Leave it to dry and stick to the glass's rim for a minute or two. You should now have a tight drum-like paper seal over the open end of the pint glass. Now carefully place a 5p or 1p coin in the centre of the taut paper. As long as you have sealed the paper well, the coin should rest there easily without making the paper sag too much.

Playing

Light a cigarette. It *must* be a packet cigarette not a roll up as the sulphur in straights will keep the cigarette burning, *without* you actually having to smoke it. Players take it in turns to burn at least the area of a cigarette end through the toilet paper. This does not have to be done by burning a single hole. It could be lots of small burns, but everyone playing must agree that you have burnt at least the square area of one cigarette end. You can burn more than the area of the end of a cigarette if you're feeling confident. Soon the coin will be held by an everdecreasing amount of paper. The player who burns their hole and makes the coin drop has to finish their drink. The loser must also pick the coin out of the ash in the glass. The game is then reset for another **round**[2].

INFO+ If you intend playing seemless multiple rounds[2], then it is best to prepare a number of glasses with toilet paper before you start the first game.

Chapter 5
Skill Games

This is the Witch

Brief description

Pass something you **call**[7] the Witch around the circle following rules specifying what you may say as you receive or pass it on. It will all get very confusing!

Number of players

More than three players.

Situation

A noisy place is not recommended as **calls**[1] must be heard.

Drinks needed

Any

Difficulty

Easy

INFO+ The game does get confusing after the **go** has been passed round a few times.

Intoxication level

Low

Implements needed

An object which is big enough to be noticed but small enough to be passed around easily. An empty **beer** bottle is perfect and is the Witch in the example below.

Shelf life ☆☆☆

'This is the Witch' is **a great (G)**! However it lacks the competition aspect which gives other games their longevity. After a few **rounds²** it becomes too familiar and gets to be too easy. Nevertheless, when you're in the company of novice players on another occasion you'll reincarnate 'This is the Witch' and wonder "Why did I ever get bored of it?"

The game in more detail

Player 1 starts the game by showing the Witch (the empty beer bottle) to all the players and saying clearly:

"This is the Witch."

Player 1 then looks at any other player and pretends to pass them the bottle.

Passing the Witch

However before the new keeper of the Witch (e.g. Player 2) can take the bottle he or she must say:

"The what?"

Player 1 then says convincingly, with a hint of exasperation in their voice:

"The Witch!"

Player 2 must then take the bottle and say with pretend realisation: "Ah… the Witch!"

They can now pass the Witch to anyone, including Player 1.

Now I'll show you what happens when the Witch is passed on to a new player (anyone except Player 1):

Player 2: "This is the Witch"

Player 3: "The what?"

Player 2: "The what?"

Player 1: "The Witch!"

Player 2: "The Witch!"

Player 3: "Ah… the Witch!"

The chain of questioning returns to Player 1

I hope you can see from this example that only the person who started the game knows what the Witch is. The question must always go back to the starter for confirmation of what the 'thing' is.

Now I'll show you what happens if the Witch is passed back to someone who has already had it. Any player receiving the Witch for a second time, behaves in exactly the same way as any other player who has not yet received it. This includes the Starter (i.e. Player 1).

In this example, Player 1 starts with the Witch and passes it to Player 2, who then passes it back to Player 1. The game would go as follows:

Player 1: "This is the Witch."

Player 2: "The what?"

Player 1: "The Witch!"

Player 2: "Ah… the Witch!"

Player 2: "This is the Witch."

Player 1: "The what?"

Player 2: "The what?"

Player 1: "The Witch!"

Player 2: "The Witch!"

Player 1: "Ah… the Witch!"

Confused yet?

Just remember only the very first player knows what the Witch is. Any time the Starter or any other player is told, "This is the Witch," they must ask what it is. The chain of questioning always goes back to the Starter, and passes through every player who has had the Witch.

I'm Colonel Puff

a.k.a Captain Pat

Brief description

Players learn and perform a sequence of words and actions to finish a whole pint. Any mistake in the sequence will mean that they finish their original drink and then start again with a whole new pint. Each player will be punished in this fashion for as long as it takes them to learn and perform the sequence of actions correctly.

Number of players

Two to six players. You can play with more, but as players take turns to learn a sequence of movements later players will find the sequence easier to learn and consequently provide less entertainment.

Situation

It must be reasonably quiet to hear the **calls**[1]. Definitely a pre-going **out**[2] game (**pre-lash (P)**). This game will finish off drinks for you as the volume of liquid consumed is high. An **everything wet must go (E)** game.

Drinks needed

Lots of **beer** or cider.

Difficulty

Medium

INFO+ The sequence of movements is difficult to learn – that's the idea. However, the game itself is simple and *The Lash* will allow you as the **Administrator** to learn the movements at your leisure.

Intoxication level

High

INFO+ Especially if it's your first time playing. Get a couple of things wrong and you're going to be **downing** pint after pint of gassy beer or cider.

Implements needed

A table, a chair each and a pint.

Shelf life ☆☆☆

Unfortunately this is one of those games which learned once can't be played with the same friends again. The fun of this game is in fining those players who get the sequence wrong.

The game in more detail

This is a game you as the **Boss** or Administrator need to learn and then inflict on others who are beginners. Start the game by explaining that:

"Players must endure their turn to the *very end* no matter what it takes!"

You then say:

"I am going to show you how to become 'Colonel Puff,' very slowly, once, and only once, so pay *very close attention!*"

You then perform a perfect demonstration of the following, slowly explaining (i.e. **coaching**) as you go.

Set up

First of all you should be sitting on a chair at a table with your drink within arm's reach and say:

First sequence

1. "I'm Colonel Puff drinking for the *first* time this evening." (Change "this evening" depending on when you're playing.)

You're set, ready to play

2. Hold out both index fingers and close the rest of your fingers in a fist. Tap both fingers *once* on the top of the table and *once* on the underside of the table.

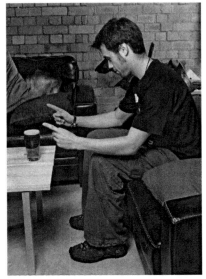

One tap above with one finger   **One tap below with one finger**

3. Sit up *once* in the chair, i.e. take your bum off the seat and sit back down again.

4. Nod *once*.

5. Pick up your drink with only your index finger and thumb, i.e. *one* finger and thumb.

6. Take *one* sip.

7. Bang the pint back down on the table *once*... and the sequence now continues into Puff Puff.

Second sequence
1. "I'm Colonel Puff Puff drinking for the *second* time this evening." (or whenever)

2. Hold out both index fingers and both the fingers next to the index finger and close the rest of your fingers in a fist on both hands, like a **blessing sign (B)**.

Tap all four fingers *twice* on the top of the table and *twice* on the underside of the table.

Double tap above with two fingers

Double tap below with two fingers

3. Sit up and down *twice* in the chair, i.e. take your bum off the seat *twice*.

4. Nod *twice*.

5. Pick up your drink with index finger, middle finger and thumb, i.e. *two* fingers and thumb.

6. Take *two* sips.

7. Bang the pint back down on the table *twice*… and the sequence now continues into Puff Puff Puff.

Third sequence
1. "I'm Colonel Puff Puff Puff drinking for the *third and final* time this evening." (or whenever)

2. Hold out your forefinger, middle finger and ring finger on both hands. Keep your **pinkies** and thumbs tucked in so you're making a **scout's sign (S)**. Tap all six fingers *three* times on the top of the table and *three* times on the underside of the table.

Triple tap above with three fingers

Triple tap below with three fingers

3. Sit up and down *three* times in the chair, i.e. take your bum off the seat *three* times.

4. Nod *three* times.

5. Pick up your drink with all fingers except the pinky aided by the thumb, i.e. *three* fingers and thumb.

6. Take *three* sips. On the third sip your glass should be empty.

7. Bang the empty pint glass back down on the table *three* times.

Well done! You have proved yourself worthy to be **called**[7] 'Colonel Puff the Third'.

INFO+ At the start of the sequence you should have a full drink and by the end an empty glass. You have six sips during the sequence to finish your drink, so pace yourself, you don't want to leave yourself a lot of work on the last sip.

You have probably realised that in the first sequence everything is done once, in the second sequence everything is done twice and in the third sequence everything is done three times. A simple rule to remember, but you'll be surprised how often players get things wrong.

At the end of the coaching sequence say: "It's over to you now but be warned that **no mercy rules (M)** now apply." This means that no help can be offered, not even from you as the Administrator and mistakes are always punished ruthlessly. Any player who makes a mistake in the sequence will have to finish their drink and go back to the beginning of the sequence with a fresh drink. Let them learn by experience. Players will have to work out what they did wrong themselves and may keep making the same mistake. I find a **repeat offender (R)** very amusing!

You now oversee each player in turn attempting to become 'Colonel Puff the Third'. Only when the whole sequence is complete does the **go** pass on to the next player. Later players will have had more demonstrations, so in theory should be more likely to finish first time.

Common mistakes to watch out for from beginners
- not remembering that they are first 'Puff' then 'Puff Puff' and then 'Puff Puff Puff' when they introduce themselves at the start of each sequence
- not tapping the glass on the table the specified number of times at the end of each **round**[2].

INFO+ Not tapping the glass is particularly fun to **pick up on (P)** when it is incorrectly performed because the offender will believe they have just finished a round[2]. Or the most entertaining scenario for you, they will think they have completely finished and then you send them right back to the start. You will see the **cocky** look fall from their face when they realise their mistake!

Players can take the sequence in their own time, though overly hesitant or slow performers should be chastised so that they speed up.

Beer Pong

Brief description
Make your opposition drink by throwing a ping pong ball into the cups of drink arranged at their end of the table.

Number of players
Two or four players.

Situation
A great game for a BBQ, although you need plenty of room. Not one for a fine drinking establishment.

Drinks needed
Lots of **beer** or cider.

Difficulty
Easy

INFO+ This is not difficult to understand. A degree of skill is needed to play.

Intoxication level
High

INFO+ The more cups you lay out, the higher the intoxication level.

Implements needed
A long table, a ping pong ball and small plastic cups.

Shelf life ☆☆☆
Addictive

The game in more detail
At either end of a long table, the best sort is a **trestle table (T)**, set up the small plastic cups in a triangular pattern like pool balls. The base of the triangle is parallel with the end of the table.

Cup formation at the start of the game

Taking aim

INFO+ Some rules for 'Beer Pong' state that you cannot lean over the table. I say, make your own rules as you see fit.

Make the same arrangement of cups at each end of the table. Now fill the cups with beer or cider.

This game is very simple. If you're playing 1 vs 1, then Player 1 will stand at their end of the table and throw the ping pong ball, in an attempt to get it in one of Player 2's cups. The ball must *not* bounce. It can touch the rim of the cup but *must not* use the table. If the ball goes in then Player 2 must drink the contents of that cup. If Player 1 misses with their throw then they must drink one of their own cups. Empty cups are removed.

An optional **call**[1] is to nominate exactly which cup you will hit with your throw. If you then proceed to get it in the one you nominated then your competitor at the other end of the table will have to drink and remove two cups from the table. However, if you arrogantly nominate a cup and either get it in another cup or miss completely then you must drink and remove two of your own cups. Opposing players take it in turns to throw and you only get one throw on your go. Each time a cup or cups are removed the triangle formation is rearranged so that there are no gaps in the pattern. The winning player is the last person to have cups on the table. The loser then has to drink the contents of the winner's cups. For doubles, players at each end take turns to throw and down drinks.

Other rules

'Beer Pong' is a world renowned drinking game which is particularly big in the United States. Some people there even consider it a sport! There are lots of official and unofficial rules. One of the main additions to my version is the bounced shot (one or more bounces) which like a nominated shot is worth two cups as it is more difficult. Rules also exist for defending cups from throws, although I believe that in the spirit of *The Lash* this should not be encouraged. I believe you should just submit yourself to a good throw and accept your fate!

It's best to play a little and decide what works best for you. It depends whether you're seeing this as a sport or a way to get battered (see **pissed**). For more on this gaming phenomenon **check out (C²)** the Internet.

Cointap

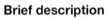

Brief description
Players tap their coins on the table in turn. Different taps switch the order of play.

Number of players
Four players or more.

Situation
You must be able to hear a coin tap on a table, so nowhere too noisy. You will also need a table on which you won't mind getting a few coin marks.

Drinks needed
Anything you're drinking.

Difficulty
Medium
INFO+ Not difficult to play, though watch out for those **gear changes (G)** (see p52).

Intoxication level
Medium

Implements needed
Everyone must have a coin, the larger the better. You must be sat around a sturdy table which has an accessible top and underside.

Shelf life ☆☆☆
A really great game! Frequently used, however once everyone learns how to play, the game will become less enjoyable.

The game in more detail
Sit round a table with your friends. You start the game by tapping your coin quickly and rhythmically on top of the table and at the command "Tune your instruments!" all the other players follow suit.

Tune your instruments!

When everyone is tapping, you tap your coin once with emphasis, louder than the fast tapping. The game has now begun and everyone stops tapping. The **go** will now **move off (M)** to the left on top of the table. The game always begins in this way, i.e. to the left.

The player to the left of the starter can now choose:
- to tap the top of the table with their coin *once* (this sends the go on in the direction it is moving, i.e. to the left)
- or to tap the table twice (this will **flip reverse (F)** the order, i.e. the go returns to the player on the right on the other side of the table).

To recap: one tap sends the go on, in the same direction and on the same side of the table. Two taps reverses the direction of the go and changes the side of the table.

If the go is already under the table when it comes to you, one tap under the table will keep it going the same way round the circle on the underside. Two taps in this scenario will flip the go onto the top side of the table and reverse the direction.

Once everyone understands the single and double tap, you can introduce that 'three taps skips a go'. The side of the table is not altered by a skip so if you're on the underside, the go remains on that side of the table.

Mistakes

Any hesitation on your go will result in a fine. Likewise, any goes which are out of turn or use the wrong table surface will be punished. If a player is confused as to which side of the table is correct, they could witness gear changes. If you spot a gear change, point it out and impose a suitable fine. This will be very amusing for all concerned.

I'll show you a quick example game:

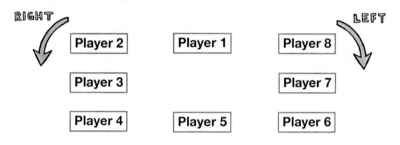

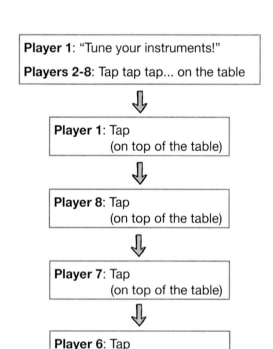

Player 5: Tap tap
(on top of the table)

Player 6: Tap
(underside of the table)

Player 7: Tap
(underside of the table)

Player 8: Tap
(underside of the table)

Player 1: Tap tap
(underside of the table)

Player 8: Tap
(on top of the table)

Player 7: Tap tap tap
(on top of the table)

Player 5: Tap tap
(on top of the table)

Player 6: Tap tap tap
(underside of the table)

Player 8: Tap (underside of the table)

Player 1: Tap (underside of the table)

Player 2: Tap (underside of the table)

Player 3: Tap tap (underside of the table)

Player 2: Tap (on top of the table)

Touch the Cup

Brief description
At the start of your **go** contribute as much or as little of your drink as you like to the communal cup. Next you try to bounce a two pence coin into the cup. You can move the cup but you must say "Touch the cup" before you touch it and you must never slide the cup. If you get the coin in, you nominate someone to drink what is currently in the cup and make up a new rule for the game. After this it is your go again to contribute and bounce.
INFO+ See the coin hit the cup at *www.thelash.eu*

Number of players
Three players or more.

Situation
Pre-lash (P) but you must be able to hear each other say "Touch the cup."

Drinks needed
Anything alcoholic.

Difficulty
Hard
INFO+ Not difficult to understand but it's difficult to become proficient at bouncing the coin.

Intoxication level
High

Implements needed
A tall, wide-rimmed coffee cup (a normal-sized **Starbucks** cup) or similar, which is used as the communal cup or **pot**. You also need a two pence piece.

Shelf life ☆☆☆☆
High

The game in more detail

Sit round a table. Before you start playing properly take the two pence coin and conduct a couple of trail bounces to test the table's bounce-ability. The go always moves left round the group. In this game the idea is for you on your go to bounce the two pence coin into the communal cup.

The rules of the game
Rule 1 – Touch the cup

Before touching the cup, you must always say "Touch the cup". Anyone can say "Touch the cup" and then touch it but you would only generally need to touch it on your go in order to bring it nearer to you. If you touch the cup without saying "Touch the cup" then your fine is to drink whatever is in the cup at that time and then give the cup back to the player who last had the go.

Rule 2 – No sliding of the cup

You should never slide the cup, only cleanly pick it up and put it down. Your fine is to drink whatever is in the cup at that time and then give the cup back to the player whose go it was before your misdemeanour.

Rule 3 – Don't accept the coin unless it's slid across the table

Passing on the go has a rule attached to it. No player can receive a coin in the air, i.e. passed from hand to hand. It can only be accepted when it has been slid across the table. You are allowed to try and catch out other players when passing the go but if you are not successful (i.e. the next player does not accept the passed coin) then you may be **called**[4] for bad etiquette by any player including the player to whom you have just attempted to pass the coin. If you are called[4] for bad etiquette, you will be fined by the player next to you, i.e. the one you tried to **stitch up (S)** (they may not be very merciful on your fine seeing as you tried to trick them). After you have accepted and taken your punishment, it is the go of the player who just fined you. What are the chances if they get the coin in the cup they're going to **call**[5] you to drink? Pretty high I'd say!

However, if you are successful and the player next to you to accepts a passed coin, then make the other players aware of the **faux pas (F)**. The player who accepted the passed coin will be fined as their punishment. It is still their go after the fine. Therefore, I'd say that if they get the coin in the cup, it's likely you'll be drinking! Trying to pass the coin is rarely attempted as it is seen as un-gentlemanly and is likely to make you enemies.

Rule 4 – Bad fielding

There is one more special rule associated with the game. If a coin is bounced and it flies off the table, the nearest player to where the coin left the table is fined whatever is in the cup for bad fielding. After the punishment has been taken, it is the wayward bouncer's go again. You have to use your discretion with this rule as someone bouncing the coin cannot be deliberately looking to bounce it off the table in the direction of a player they want to drink. If this is the case, fine the bouncer.

These four rules stand throughout the game and cannot be overidden by any new rule created in the course of the game.

Playing

Before you bounce the coin on your go, you contribute as much or as little drink to the communal cup as you like. This depends, as in the game 'Arrogance' (p26), on how confident you are about getting the coin in. If you don't manage to bounce the coin in you'll drink what you have contributed yourself. After making your contribution, if you bounce the coin and get it straight in the cup you nominate any other player you like to drink what is currently in the cup. You also get to make up a new rule for the game.

Making new rules

A new rule is in effect throughout the game and only expires when another rule is specially created to cancel it.

You can make up any rules you like but here are some ideas:
- on receiving the coin for their go the player must nod their head. If they forget then they are fined. You can replace the nod with any action or sound. Receiving the coin is one of the formalities of the game and the action or sound will happen every time the go moves on. The action or sound becomes part of the ceremony of the game and it's easy to spot if it gets left out
- no swearing (you'll find this difficult once everyone has had a few drinks). Any expletives are fined
- **no pointing (P)** with fingers – you'll be surprised how hard this can be. Pointing with your elbow is acceptable and will look highly comical
- left-handed drinking (simple but effective). Anyone who drinks with their right hand has **buffaloed**. If you see this happen shout "Buffalo!" The player is fined.

What happens if you break the rules?

If any player breaks any rule at any point, for example by touching the cup without saying "Touch the cup", the go passes directly to the rule breaker and they drink what ever is in the cup before the go returns to the correct player. If the player just fined offends again immediately, it is up to the player whose go it is to pour a repeat fine into the cup.

The Nomination

If you get the coin in the cup, you can nominate any player to drink. The idea is to bully other players. Once you have nominated and the player of your choice has drunk, it is your go to bounce again. If a player is proficient at the bouncing skill they can keep dishing out drink and making up rules. A fun tactic if this is the case, is to pick on one person in particular!

Challenge rule

If you hit the rim but the coin falls outside the cup, then any other player can say "Challenge." After a 'challenge' call[6] the player whose go it was has their go again and must make a new contribution to the cup. This contribution should be a decent amount, similar to the amount they put in before the 'Challenge'.

Possible outcomes of a 'Challenge'

Player gets the coin in: If the player whose go it is manages to get the coin into the cup on the re-try, (basically a **double or bust (D)** situation) then the person who called[6] the 'Challenge' drinks what's in the cup. The go then passes on one place to the left of the player challenged.

Player doesn't get the coin in: If the challenged player does not get the coin in, then they drink what's in the cup. The go passes on one place to the left of the player challenged.

Repeat challenge: If the challenged player hits the rim again then it's an **auto re-challenge (A)** by the challenger. Another contribution is made and the challenged player tries to bounce the coin in again. You may realise that if you keep hitting the rim, the cup can become a very daunting proposition!

Drink Bowling

Brief description
This is a **team outing (O⁴)** which will get very **messy**. Basically you **go** bowling in the normal way but the number of pins you leave standing on each go is the number of **fingers** of drink you are fined. If you get a spare (that's the / sign on the big screen) then the next person to roll after you must throw one ball with their weaker arm. If you hit a strike (that's the X sign on the big screen) then the next person to roll after you must throw both balls with their weaker arm.

Number of players
You could play with two players but you want plenty of friends for a successful evening.

Situation
You and your friends take the **pre-lash (P)** on **tour** to a bowling alley. Loud, public and entertaining!

Coming to a bowling alley near you!

Drinks needed
Usually pints of lager, and loads of it!

Difficulty
Easy

INFO+ Easy, though depends what your bowling is like. Please don't play with **bumpers** or you will look really **lame**.

Intoxication level
Extreme

Implements needed
A nearby bowling alley with a bar. You can also play this with **skittles** which you'll find in more **yokel** pubs.

Shelf life ☆☆☆☆
If you thought bowling was just for your tenth birthday party, think again!

The game in more detail
Go to your local bowling alley and order as much drink from the bar as your wallet can handle, owwr even better, press the waiter service button and have someone bring you the drinks. In bowling, on any one normal go, you get two chances to throw a ball to knock down the ten pins because there are ten after all! In 'Drink Bowling' each pin left standing is a fine of a finger of your drink. Therefore the aim of the game if you don't want to get totally **wasted** is to knock down as many pins as possible. The maximum fine that you could get on any one **round**[2] is ten fingers because there are ten pins. Given that eight fingers is a pint, that's almost a litre of drink you'll have to consume if you fail to hit any pins on your go. If you're thinking "That doesn't sound that difficult!" then see the rules below because they might give you problems!

Rules
A spare
If the person before you gets a spare (that's the / sign on the big screen), you must bowl one of the balls on your go with your weaker throwing arm. It doesn't matter whether it is the first or the second ball you throw with the weaker arm.

A strike

If the person before you gets a strike (that's the X sign on the big screen), you must bowl both balls on your go with your weaker arm. This might lead to abysmal bowling and a big fine.

If any players are truly ambidextrous, then good luck to them. In my experience few people really are, even if they profess to be!

INFO+ You might have already realised that it's a good tactic to ensure that you're not after a strong bowler in the order of play. To guarantee the place you want, make sure that you're the person who puts the names into the computer at the start. If lots of people playing recognise that it's not beneficial to go after a strong bowler then work out the bowling order by picking names out of a hat. This prevents arguments and ensures relative fairness. Good luck!

Chapter 6
Card Games

 ## Stop the Bus!

Brief description

All players have a playing card stuck to their foreheads. They count off round the table. When a player calls "Stop the bus!" the player with the highest card and the player who 'stopped the bus' drink.

Number of players

Too many players and the game will not complete a whole **round**[2], too few and fines can increase very quickly. Six players is probably the perfect number.

Situation

If you have a pack of cards the game can be played anywhere.

Drinks needed

Anything you're drinking at the time of playing. Fines can build quickly so have enough drink in front of you: a pint should be adequate.

Difficulty
Easy

Intoxication level
Medium

Implements needed

A pack of cards.

Shelf life ☆☆☆

This can lose its excitement after a couple of rounds[2] but is enjoyable whilst the novelty persists.

The game in more detail

All players gather in a circle. Every player must be able to see every other player. Deal out one card from a shuffled pack, face down to each player. Players *must not* look at their cards. Instead they each lick the back of the card and stick it to their forehead. This rather silly look enables every player to see every other player's cards whilst no player can see their own.

Silly but functional — sticking the cards to your forehead

The idea is that the player with the highest card will always pay the fine. How much the fine will amount to, or who will be joining the player with the highest card in the fine, is decided by the game. The fine always starts on one **finger**. For every completed round another finger of drink is added on to the fine.

How does the game proceed?

You start the game by either saying "One," or "Stop the bus!" You're unlikely to say "Stop the bus," at this stage unless you think you have the highest card, so the most likely **call**[1] is "One." Player 2 then says either "Two," or "Stop the bus!" If everyone counts, the game continues round the whole circle of players and will eventually return to Player 1 (the Starter). The fine now goes up to two fingers for the person with the highest card.

What happens if you say 'Stop the bus'?

If you say "Stop the bus!" on your **go** the game stops and everyone takes off their card. If the highest card *is* you, then you alone will take the fine. If you do *not* have the highest card then you will join the person with the highest card in taking the fine. This rule encourages players not to call[1] "Stop the bus!" too early and allows the level of fine to rise.

Calculating the fine

In an example game with six players the fines would mount as follows:

On the first round the fine is one finger. When the count reaches seven (when the go returns to Player 1) the fine will be two fingers of drink and so on.

The **Administrator** should hold one finger up on the first round[2] and add another finger to the hand tally for every complete circle of goes.

Eye contact, a.k.a looks or glances

In the game you will find that as the fine increases, players will not be able to prevent themselves from looking at the player with the highest card on their head. This will make the player with the high card suspicious and thus more likely to 'stop the bus' on their go to limit their fine.

Dummy looks can be used to make people call[1] "Stop the bus!" (thus incurring a fine they shouldn't have had to drink) and can put the player with the highest card **off the scent (S)**. Although of course if the fine is really **racking up (R)**, **a good samaritan (S)** might help the player with the highest card out, by staring at them. You cannot signal to the player with the highest card although looking at their card is allowed. You'll notice that in 'Stop the Bus!' there are glances flying everywhere.

Fines can reach epic proportions if all players stubbornly believe they don't have the highest card and keeps counting.

In this example game I have shown you all the players' cards. In real games, of course, players wouldn't know their own card.

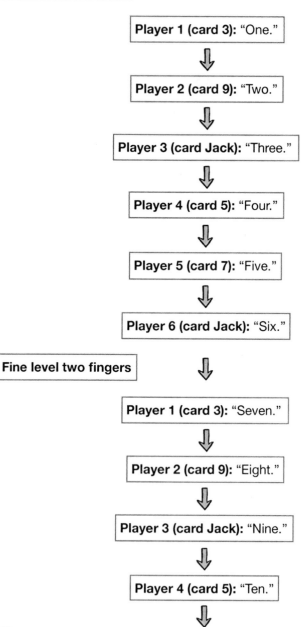

Fine level one finger

Player 1 (card 3): "One."

Player 2 (card 9): "Two."

Player 3 (card Jack): "Three."

Player 4 (card 5): "Four."

Player 5 (card 7): "Five."

Player 6 (card Jack): "Six."

Fine level two fingers

Player 1 (card 3): "Seven."

Player 2 (card 9): "Eight."

Player 3 (card Jack): "Nine."

Player 4 (card 5): "Ten."

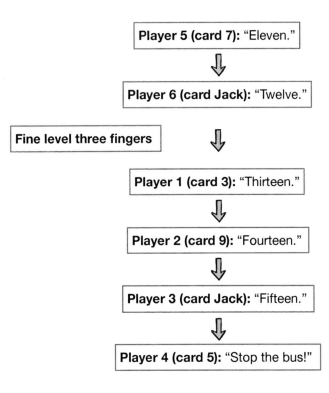

Player 5 (card 7): "Eleven."

⬇

Player 6 (card Jack): "Twelve."

Fine level three fingers   ⬇

Player 1 (card 3): "Thirteen."

⬇

Player 2 (card 9): "Fourteen."

⬇

Player 3 (card Jack): "Fifteen."

⬇

Player 4 (card 5): "Stop the bus!"

The resolution of the fines
In the example above, Player 4 will be fined three fingers of drink for stopping the game and not being the highest card. Players 3 and 6 will also take their fine of three fingers each for having the joint highest cards.

A good saying for this game is "**A quick game's a good game! (Q)**" Make sure the counting is quick and the fines are administered promptly. The quicker the game, the more quickly the fines rack up as players don't have time to consider whether they really should be continuing to count.

At the end of a game and after the fines have been taken, cards pass to Player 2 and they reshuffle and deal to restart the game. The game starts as before except the first call[1] (i.e. to count or say "Stop the bus!") is with Player 2 and Player 1 calls[1] last.

Pyramid

Brief description

Each player is dealt a card and a pyramid of cards is set out face down on the table. Cards from the pyramid are turned over one by one. If the suit or number matches any player's cards they are fined. Fines get worse towards the pinnacle of the pyramid.

Number of players

It is possible to play with two players, however I recommend six or more.

Situation

Before you go **out**[2], so **pre-lash (P)** or at a house party.

Drinks needed

Anything you're drinking though you'll need lots of it!

Difficulty

Easy

Intoxication level

High

Implements needed

A pack of cards.

Shelf life ☆☆☆☆

You'll come back to this game but not straightaway, unless you've got a **head tap (H)**.

The game in more detail

Deal every player a card from a shuffled pack. They should show this card to all other players and they can look at it themselves. I suggest licking the card on the back and sticking it to your forehead, as in the game 'Stop the Bus!' (p163). This way everyone can see it clearly.

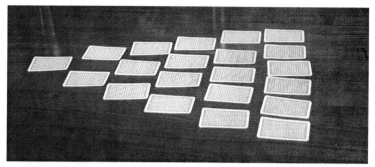

Pyramid with six rows

Make a pyramid (on the floor or table) of face down cards using the rest of the pack. Start with a single card followed by a row of two cards below, followed by a row of three cards, etc. After row three you don't have to strictly follow the pattern of having one more card in each row. Don't have more than six or seven rows otherwise the fining system won't work (see below). Any remaining cards stay in the pack unknown and are not used in the game.

Be like Brucey!
In this game you are the Card Turner or Card Master, a.k.a. **Bruce Forsyth (F)**. As the Card Turner you also play in the game and must have a card.

Starting the game
The game starts and the first card to be turned is the one furthest left on the bottom row (the row with the most cards).

The game begins!

The Card Master turns over one card at a time from left to right on each row. The fine for matching cards depends on which row the card came from.

Let's say the pyramid has six rows of cards. Row 1 is the single card at the pinnacle and row 6 has the most cards.

Fines
Row 6 = One finger
Row 5 = Two fingers
Row 4 = Three fingers
Row 3 = Four fingers
Row 2 = Half your drink **in one (O)**
Row 1 = **Down** your drink in one

More than one player can be fined. For example, if a 5 of Diamonds is turned on row 4 and the players' cards are as follows...

Player 1: Jack of Diamonds
Player 2: 10 of Spades
Player 3: 3 of Hearts
Player 4: 5 of Clubs

Player 5: Ace of Diamonds
Player 6: 5 of Spades
Player 7: Queen of Hearts
Player 8: 3 of Diamonds

... then Players 1, 5 and 8 must drink for holding diamonds, and Players 4 and 6 drink for holding fives. Each player drinks three fingers. Fines must be taken in full before the next card in the pyramid is turned by you, the Card Master.

The higher or lower '*Play Your Cards Right*' add on

To make 'Pyramid' more exciting you can also include a go after each card is turned. The go passes round the players in sequence and on your go you must decide whether the next card will be higher or lower than the previous card. If you make the wrong prediction, for example you say higher and it's lower, you are fined as on a normal go. If the card is the same value as the one before then you are also fined.

INFO+ If you are playing 'higher and lower' you could get the prediction wrong, and also have the matching number or suit for the card that is turned. You would then would be liable for double the standard fine at that level of the 'Pyramid'.

There are several variations of 'Pyramid'. If you like this, **check out (C²)** 'Pyramid Cheat', which is currently my favourite drinking game.

Pyramid Cheat

Brief description
Each player is dealt three cards, face down. Players have three seconds to look at and memorise their three cards before putting them down. As with 'Pyramid' (p168) the Card Master lays out cards in a pyramid formation and turns them over one at a time. Any player who has, or claims to have a card of equal value to the new card can nominate another player to drink a fine.

A player can accept the fine distributed to them or **call**[6] the player who imposed it on them a 'cheat'. Anyone who is called a cheat must prove themselves by turning over the card in their own hand that matches the one in the pyramid. This is a subtle game of **bluff** and tactics – **a great (G)** to enjoy!

INFO+ The cheat idea in this game is taken from the popular card game of the same name. If you know 'Cheat!' then you'll already have the skill set to be successful at this game.

Number of players
You can play with two players but six makes for an entertaining game.

Situation
Pre-lash (P) or house party. Not suitable for a busy pub.

Drinks needed
Anything you're drinking, though lots of it.

Difficulty
Complex

INFO+ Lots of tactics are involved in this game. The game basics are easily understood. It is the fining that may seem complicated when written down but in practice you'll find it more straightforward.

Intoxication level
Extreme

INFO+ Fines can really mount up quickly.

Implements needed
A pack of cards.

Shelf life ☆☆☆☆
You'll come back to this game again and again but probably not on the same day.

The game in more detail
A few points to make clear before I get on with the explanation of how to play:

- fines are per card – if you have three queens you have three **lots** of fine to distribute
- fines cannot be broken down into composite **fingers**. Fines are taken in lots, which can be added together but never broken down. For example, if on row 3 a player says, "I have two queens," this means they have two lots of four fingers to distribute. This could be give as eight fingers to one player or as two lots of four fingers to two different players. You cannot give two fingers to one player and two fingers to another as this would involve breaking lots
- if your call[6] someone to drink, you must point at the card or cards you claim to have in your set of three on the table
- you cannot call[6] someone a cheat if they are not making you drink. This is the most important rule.

Making the pyramid
After dealing three cards to each player, lay out a pyramid, using the remaining cards, in the centre of the playing area. Any remaining cards are set aside.

INFO+ After row 3 you don't have to strictly follow the pattern of having one more card on each row. Don't have more than six or seven rows for the fines, as they will become rather silly. See the photo for the arrangement of cards in the pyramid.

The three cards in front of you
Every player has three cards. They do not show anyone else these cards. Everyone looks at their own cards at the same time in a three second frenzy of memorising.

The pyramid is laid out and all players have their three cards. Now it's time to quickly memorise your cards and then place them face down on the table again

It is best to count all players in: "1, 2, 3... look at your cards!" You then give everyone three seconds to look at their cards. During this period you will also be trying to remember your own three cards! Then say "Right put them back!"

Players must not look at their cards again at any point during the game. The only time you can turn a card is if you are challenged as a cheat! If you pick the wrong card when asked to show it, you will be fined.

Fines

Fines are allotted by any player who has, or claims to have, a card matching the one turned over by the Card Master.

e.g. the Card Master turns over a queen.

Player 1: "I have a queen, Player 2 please drink one finger."

If Player 1 had two queens he or she could ask two other players to drink a finger each or give two fingers to one player.

Row	Fine amount to distribute if say "I have... card(s)"	Position/number of cards on the row
6	One finger	The bottom row with the most cards
5	Two fingers	Five or more cards but less cards than row 6
4	Three fingers	Four or more cards but less cards than row 5
3	Four fingers	Three cards
2	Half your drink **in one (O)**	Two cards
1	**Down** your drink in one	The pinnacle (one card only)

Options on receiving a fine

I will call[6] the player receiving the fine(s) the Finee and the player giving the fine(s) the Distributor.

Any player who is asked to drink a fine has two options:

Option 1

Accept the fine and drink the amount specified. If you do this you are accepting that the Distributor has the card(s) they have or that you realise the **stakes** are too high to risk doubling or tripling the basic fine by calling[6] the Distributor a 'cheat'.

Option 2

Call[6] the Distributor a 'cheat!' Remember, you cannot call[6] someone a 'cheat!' if they are not making you drink. If the Finee says "Cheat!" then the Distributor must prove they have the card(s) they claim to have by turning one, two or three of their set of three cards. The card or cards turned in the set of three by the Distributor must correspond with the card turned in the pyramid. If the Distributor's card or cards do not match the card turned in the pyramid, because they're lying or have made an incorrect selection, they will take double the amount of fine for each incorrect card.

However if the cards do match up and the Finee has made an incorrect 'Cheat' call[6] then the Finee's fine will double. If two or more players pick the same Finee then the Finee can call[6] 'cheat' to one player, both or neither.

Showing cards

The Distributor must show the number of cards they said they had, even if they have admitted to lying. By calling[6] 'cheat' a player has **paid**, as in **Poker**, to see someone's cards. The potential Finee has paid by taking the risk of doubling their fine. Once a card has been revealed it is placed face down again.

INFO+ Players should try and remember all cards that are revealed for future reference.

Can a card be shown more than once?

Cards that have been shown are not redundant. They can be used again to issue fines and for bluffing. If you're bluffing on cards that have already been shown, you'd better be sure the player you're giving the fine to has a poor memory!

INFO+ At this point you have enough information to start playing. However, if you want to understand the intricacies of the betting to gain a full appreciation for 'Pyramid Cheat', then read on.

What happens if you have more than one of the cards revealed in the pyramid, should you want to pretend you have them?

If you say you have two cards like the one revealed in the pyramid the initial fine is doubled. If you say you have three it's tripled. Of course any player can say they have two queens or even three. You don't actually have to have the cards but you may need to be good at bluffing to pull off the ruse!

Let's look at some possible scenarios:

Scenario 1

A queen is turned on row 6 (one finger fine level). Player 1 has multiple queens.

Player 1: "I have two queens. Player 4, please drink one finger and Player 5 please also drink one finger."

Or in the case of a very rare situation or a brazen bluff:
Player 1: "I have three queens. Player 4, Player 5 and Player 2 please drink one finger."

The player who says they have the card which was turned can distribute the fines in any way they like as long as they keep fine lots together. They could put two or three times the fine on a single player if they want to **stitch them up (S)**. For example:

Player 1: "I have two queens. Player 3 drink two fingers."

Scenario 2

This scenario illustrates why it is so important that you specify which cards you are making use of when distributing fines. A queen is turned on row 3, Player 1 has only one queen.

Player 1: "I've got two queens. Player 2 drink four fingers and Player 3 drink four fingers."

Player 2 challenges Player 1 ("Cheat!") but Player 3 drinks. As no card was specified, Player 1 is able to turn over a queen from their three cards and make Player 2 drink.

Can you see why this situation is unfair?

Player 2 was unfairly disadvantaged because no card was specified by Player 1. Player 1 therefore manages to avoid a fine with just one queen when actually he or she was claiming to have two.

Player 1 should have pointed at one card as they challenged Player 2 and one as they challenged Player 3. The one revealed to Player 2 should have been the one that was pointed at.

Scenario 3

A five is turned on row 4 (three-finger fine level).

Player 1: "I have two fives. Player 4 drink." (pointing at two of their three cards)

Player 2: "I have a five. Player 4 drink." (pointing at one of their three cards)

Player 4: "Right, you're both cheats! Let's see the cards!"

Player 4 has chosen to see the cards. Therefore Player 4 is taking a gamble of twelve fingers as their fine from Player 1 and a six-finger fine from Player 2.

Why twelve fingers from Player 1? Because they were on a three-finger row and there are two cards (and so two fines disputed) but this is doubled if Player 4's 'cheat' call[6] is wrong. The same stakes exist for Player 2 if they are bluffing.

Why six fingers from Player 2? The fine due from Player 2's cards was three fingers but because of the 'cheat' the stakes have been doubled.

Outcomes for scenario 3
If Player 4 is wrong on both counts they stand to drink eighteen fingers (we may have **casualty** here because that's over two pints of alcohol).

If Player 1 is cheating but Player 2 is telling the truth, then it's only six fingers for Player 4 and twelve for Player 1. If Player 1 is telling the truth and Player 2 cheating, then it's twelve fingers for Player 4 and six for Player 2. If both are cheating then it's no fingers for Player 4, six for Player 2 and twelve for Player 1.

Scenario 4
What happens if you distribute two fine lots to one player but when challenged you only have one of the cards?

A nine is turned on row 2. Player 2 has one nine. They claim to have two nines and puts both lots of fine on Player 1. Player 1 calls 'cheat'. Player 2 can only reveal one nine so has to drink two full drinks.

Why two full glasses? This is because the second row's basic fine is half your drink. Player 2 has put two lots of this fine together for the two cards so it's one full drink at this stage. However, because of the 'cheat call' the fine doubles to two completely full drinks. Oh dear, what a **savage** fine!

INFO+ This is a dangerous game and often it's better to swallow your pride and take fines, even if this means someone is lying. Be very sure in your 'cheat calls'. However, if you're bluffing a big fine onto a player or multiple players, you'll need **balls of steel (B)**!

Example game
Now let's look at an example game just to see how game play works in reality rather than via scenarios. We'll **play God (G)** and look at everyone's cards. In the game a player would only know their own three cards (if they have managed to remember them after only a quick look!)

	Each player's cards
Player 1	Ten, Eight, Seven
Player 2	King, Jack, Nine
Player 3	Two, Three, Three
Player 4	Six, Six, Two
Player 5	Queen, Six, Ten
Player 6	King, Ace, Jack
Player 7	Three, Ten, Four
Player 8	Nine, Nine, Five

The game begins on row 6, where the standard fine per card is one finger, and the first card turned is an eight.

The game begins!

Player 1: "I have an eight. Player 3 drink one finger."

Player 4: "Cheat! That's **bollocks** you haven't got an eight. Show me!"

Player 1: "Sorry (turns over pointed at card —it's an eight), Player 4 that'll be two fingers then!" The eight is then face down again.

Now I'm going to fast forward this example to the second card of row 5. The standard fine is now two fingers per card. Game on! The card turned on the pyramid is a nine.

Player 8: (pointing at two of their three face down cards) "I have two nines. Player 5 drink double the fine."

Player 2: (pointing at one of their three face down cards) "I have one nine. Player 4 drink."

Player 7: (pointing at one of their three face down cards) "I have one nine too. Player 6 drink."

Outcomes

Player 4: Drinks

Player 6: Drinks (but if you check above with your **God's eye (G)** overview of the cards, you'll see Player 6 was tricked because Player 7 doesn't have a nine)

Player 5: Calls[6] 'cheat'.

Player 8: Turns over the two nines they pointed at, much to the consternation of Player 5. Player 5 is now fined eight fingers.

Finally, if you managed to get through all that explanation in one go, you're a **legend**! It's not a difficult game but the gambling and distribution takes some explanation. Get on and play it and you'll soon realise the logic involved in the betting.

All accusations and drinking of fines must take place *before* any cards are turned. The person **bossing** the game must check that **all business is finished (B)** before the game moves on.

Gauntlet

a.k.a Crocodile or Minefield

Brief description

Try and move through a diamond arrangement of random face down cards, selecting one card per row without hitting a picture card. Sounds easy but many an intrepid challenger has failed to give 'The Gauntlet' the respect it deserves.

Number of players

Two, four, six, eight, or ten players in two teams. You don't want more than five players per side. It is possible to play with uneven numbers and this will not give any particular advantage to either side but ideally play with equal numbers on each side. This game is also good played head to head (1 vs 1).

Situation

A bar, **pre-lash (P)** or in a pub. You need a table but it doesn't matter if it's noisy where you are playing.

Drinks needed

Lots. Best to **get in (G²)** a couple of pints of lager or cider. If 'The Gauntlet' goes badly you will be consuming, in the worst case scenario, twenty **fingers** over one complete turn.

Difficulty

Medium

INFO+ Not difficult to play but it is difficult to complete 'The Gauntlet' without getting completely '**lashed**' (see **pissed** for similar terms).

Intoxication level

Extreme

INFO+ In the same group as the games 'Next!' (p9), 'Panic Button' (p14) & 'Case Race' (p5).

Implements needed

A pack of cards.

Shelf life ☆☆☆☆

If you have a competitive streak, you will want to play more than one **round**[2].

The game in more detail

The 'Gauntlet' is a diamond shape of random cards face down.

One card goes at the pinnacle (top) followed by a row of two cards followed by a row of three cards. The row of four cards is the centre point of the diamond and then a reflection of the top layout completes the diamond, i.e. three, two then one.

So the complete 'Gauntlet' will look like this:

A 'Gauntlet'

The opposing players sit facing one another with 'The Gauntlet' diamond between them. If there are multiple players, gather at either end.

To begin, first decide which player is going to challenge the 'Gauntlet', (the Contender) and who will be the Gauntlet Master/Card Layer/Card Master. This can be decided by the toss of a coin. The Gauntlet Master takes the remaining cards. The Contender's task is to get from one end of the 'Gauntlet' to the other.

The contender makes progress through the 'Gauntlet'

The Contender starts at the card which is directly in front of them and turns it over. They can pick any 'path' to the other side of the 'Gauntlet' by turning over one card on each row. If the Contender turns over a picture card they will be fined accordingly and must return to the start of the 'Gauntlet'. They can pick any card in each row, except of course in the first and last where there is no choice. The Contender is *not* required to pick a card in the next row which is adjacent to the one they turned in the row before. They could pick a card on the extreme left of row two and then a card on the extreme right of row three.

Fines

Jack	Half finger	King	One and a half fingers
Queen	Whole finger	Ace	Two fingers

In the event of a failed attempt the Contender takes their fine. The Gauntlet Master deals fresh cards to cover the Contender's path and the Contender starts again from the beginning.

The Gauntlet Master covers a failed path after the Contender hit a king on the last card. Unlucky!

If the Contender finishes the 'Gauntlet' by getting to the other side, then the players switch roles. The Contender becomes The Gauntlet Master and vice versa. To symbolise the change the old Gauntlet Master (the new Contender) passes the remaining cards to the old Contender (the new Gauntlet Master).

The changing of the guard. When the Contender reaches the end of the 'Gauntlet', the change of roles is symbolised by passing the cards

The new Gauntlet Master deals fresh cards to cover the upturned cards on the 'Gauntlet' and the game begins again.

INFO+ It is highly beneficial to finish by hitting as few picture cards as possible, not only because you will be fined less, but also because you will **stitch** your opponent as they now have a higher probability of hitting a picture card.

What happens when The Gauntlet Master runs out of cards?

When the game is coming to its conclusion, The Gauntlet Master will find that they do not have enough cards in their hand to cover over the Contender's failed path. In this event, The Gauntlet Master deals as far back up the 'Gauntlet' as possible. Any face up cards, which cannot be covered are ignored by the Contender. The Contender must pick a route via face down cards and must complete all rows in play, i.e. any with cards face down.

With The Gauntlet Master out of cards, the unlucky Contender must still turn one card on all remaining rows until he makes the end. This can be achieved by either not hitting any more picture cards or by the default of turning every card.

If the Contender is truly unlucky they might complete the 'Gauntlet' only by default, hitting every remaining card until they only have one face down card left to turn at the top of the 'Gauntlet'.

When the game finishes it is up to the Contender whether to reset the 'Gauntlet'. This is very important because if the Contender has been very unfortunate, and has done twenty fingers due to hitting every picture card on their first go, they may feel they want a chance to seek revenge on their Gauntlet Master opponent!

 # Ring of Fire

Brief description

The **go** moves round the group in one direction, left or right, for the duration of the game. This should be decided before you start. As Card Master you turn one card for each player's go. Every card from two to ace has a set consequence for the player whose go it is – from nominating another player to down their drink to all players starting on a new game within 'Ring of Fire'.

This game has taken on a reputation of **legendary** proportions in university circles. Everyone speaks of it but very few have actually played the game.

Number of players

It is best to play with more than four players. You may lose control of the game if the number of players exceeds twelve.

Situation

The ultimate game to play before you go **out**[2]. You can play it in a pub or bar if you modify the rules to suit the situation.

Drinks needed

Any

Difficulty

Medium

INFO+ The basics of this game are as simple as turning cards. However it is not the game itself that makes it difficult to play but what rule is placed on each card. You can make this game as easy or as mind-bendingly complicated as you like. Often people turn 'Ring of Fire' into the drinking game of all drinking games.

Intoxication level

High

INFO+ A difficult one to **call**[8] because it depends on what rules are placed on the cards.

Implements needed

You only need a pack of cards for 'Ring of Fire'. However, this game could require playing many other games and therefore many different implements may be needed.

Shelf life ☆☆☆☆☆

You make up new rules for every session so this game will never become old.

The game in more detail

Play with one, two or even three packs of cards. Display these cards as you turn them off the deck in a circle, spiralling in towards the centre like a snail shell.

Lay from the outside and move in to the centre in a spiral pattern

Each card in the pack means something different. Traditional rules are: the player to your left *or* right drinks or all females/males drink. Other rules can be made up by players. A fine immunity card, like a get out of jail free card in Monopoly, can be kept and used at your leisure. You can take out the jokers, or play with them so they mean a fine for everyone.

In 'Ring of Fire' it is a tradition that one card equals a certain game. When this card is turned, players play this game for a prearranged number of **rounds**[2]. You then return to the 'Ring of Fire' for the next turn of a card.

Only when the whole pack has been used up, is the game finished. If you use multiple decks this could take a whole evening's drinking.

It really is up to you how you play this game and what you make each card mean. Make sure everyone understands what each card means before playing. The best thing to do is write a quick cribsheet. If you make one card mean a certain game, make sure that you explain how to play it before the commencement of actual game play.

Here's an example of a super **savage** 'Ring of Fire' of satanic proportions:

The cards	What the card means
Ace	Play one round[2] of 'Panic Button' (p14) with a 2.5 pint jug
King	**Down** your own drink and start a game of 'Next!' (p9)
Queen	The interrogator. The player who draws this card can ask any question to any player, at any time! If anyone asked a question answers it, they are fined a **claw**. Any subsequent queen pulled out will make a new interrogator and the previous one will retire. The new interrogator is introduced to the players once and once only. Just don't forget who it is!
Jack	Nominate someone to finish their drink
Ten	Get out of jail free card. This is immunity from a fine of your choice! Keep it and be wise in its use.
Nine	Make up a new rule to be adhered to during the game
Eight	Play one round[2] of 'I Have Never...' (p112)
Seven	Play seven round[2] of 'Sevens' (p77)
Six	Dead ants! The last person to drop and play dead is fined. Pretend you're a dying ant and get on to your back, waving your arms and legs wildly in the air.
Five	Play five round[2] of 'Fives' (p31)
Four	The player to your right drinks
Three	The player to your left drinks
Two	You decide if all the males or all the females drink

The version above is **medieval**, though I always think that if you have taken the time to create a good 'Ring of Fire' sequence, you should insure the time invested is returned on your hapless friends in terms of **lash**! Nobody is leaving this game sober, or even standing. That should be your goal!

Glossary

A

Administrator

(a.k.a. the **Boss**)

Every drinking game must have an authority or leader. In *The Lash* I have called the person performing this role the Administrator. You will often be the Administrator as you will be teaching your friends the games you have learned from this book. As the Administrator it's your job to ensure the efficient running of the game. In many games you will also be called on to act as referee and dispense justice.

As the Administrator your aim is to be polite and charismatic at all times but if necessary you must be able to ensure that a player pays the fine that is due. This may make you seem harsh or even cruel in the short term. The burden of leadership is that sometimes you have to be cruel to be kind.

INFO+ See **peer pressure** for techniques to encourage reluctant participants to finish fines. Also refer to **asshole** and **cunt** for more information on the theme of tough love.

The administrator lays down the law!

Ali G

A satirical fictional character who first appeared on Channel 4's *Eleven O'Clock Show*. Alistair Leslie Graham, to quote his full name, is the brainchild of comedian Sacha Baron Cohen. The character is a stereotype of a young **urban** male whose supposedly unacceptable 'street' attitude shocks the conventionally-minded people he meets.

Ali G gets a mention in *The Lash* because of the mad 'Ali G Roman numeral 21' variant of the game '21' (p92). In this game, some of Ali G's trademark sayings are substituted for numerical symbols (see also **Roman numerals (R)**).

American Pie

A teen comedy film released in 1999. The movie follows the trials and tribulations of four soon-to-be high school graduates as they desperately attempt to lose their virginity. I have likened *The Lash* to the sex manual in *American Pie* because just like this manual, drinking games are passed down from person to person and everyone adds their own something to a drinking game. Upon finding *The Lash* you obtain the guidance to start out on your own **lash** adventures. Either read the script, *East Great Falls High* by Adam Herz, or watch *American Pie* to understand what I'm harping on about.

Ammo

Ammo is literally ordinance which is discharged from a gun. However, in *The Lash*, having ammo on someone means knowing a number of secrets about a particular person. Your memories are the bullets and your voice is the gun that will discharge these killer shots at the victim in question:

"I think you'd better shut up, because I've got loads of ammo on you!"

Ammo is utilised in 'I Have Never' (p112) and 'Paranoia' (p114) with reputation-ruining consequences!

Amoeba

The amoeba is a well-known example of a unicellular organism. The amoeba is often thought of as the smallest living organism. This may not be scientifically true but it is certainly small and it certainly moves! That's why in 'Animal Kingdom' (p130) the amoeba is always the lowest creature and starting point in the game.

Anchor leg

Anchor leg is the last person to compete in a team race. The term is most commonly used when referring to the final stretch of a relay race. The strongest runner in a team is often placed on the anchor leg to bring home the baton. I've never really understood why this makes any difference if everyone just runs as hard as they can. Maybe it's got something to do with psychology?

In the drinking game 'Boat Race' (p11), you usually put your fastest drinker on the anchor leg (i.e. they are the last to drink) so you can win in style, or at the very last moment, wrench victory from the flames of defeat.

Poor placement or lash monsters (L) in disguise? The teams' anchor legs go head to head for victory in 'Boat Race' (p11)

Asshole

An asshole is anyone who acts in a way that causes other players to dislike him or her. Sometimes an asshole is just doing their duty, but this duty is to shit on others. In your capacity as **Administrator** it may be necessary to act like an asshole in order to chastise and barrack players into accepting their fines (see also **peer pressure**). In order to maintain your authority as Administrator you will on occasions be forced to behave in a less than saintly fashion. Short-term unpopularity can come with the job.

Do not fear being an asshole for the good of the majority rather than succumbing to the selfish mentality of the individual (see **splinter** for a description of the persistently whinging drinking outcast). Think of the good of the game and you will be thanked in retrospect. For example, after taking a particularly horrendous fine, the player punished will look back on their ability to **step up (S)** to meet the challenge as an achievement. They will forget the **peer pressure** that you, as **Administrator**, were obliged to apply.

Auto re-challenge

In certain games challenges can be issued. When this happens the challenger defines the terms as it is their challenge.

However some games have a specific rule called an auto re-challenge. This is a clause that locks players into ever-increasing **stakes** if a certain event happens repeatedly (e.g. the coin hitting the rim of the glass over and over again in 'Touch the Cup' (p155)). Auto re-challenges are non-negotiable, as they are part of the rules of the game.

Under certain conditions fines can spiral out of control, often against the will of players involved and much to the amusement of all those who are not involved in the unfolding situation. Auto re-challenges can happen consecutively for an infinite number of times doubling, tripling, quadrupling or multiplying even more times than the initial fine.

One game in which auto re-challenges are ever-present is 'Touch the Cup' (p155). I would advise you tread carefully with challenges in this game for by making an initial challenge you may end up risking a much higher fine.

B

Bagsy

To 'bagsy' is to claim something for yourself, e.g. "Bagsy the back seat on the bus!" This works in the same way as **shotgun** in that the first person to say 'bagsy' and the name of the thing they want, gets it. This is a rather childish way to solve sharing issues, but I have to say, it is effective! It basically means that the person most **on the ball (B)** can claim whatever they desire. I have only one rule that limits the bagsy rule and that is you cannot bagsy members of the opposite sex (or the same sex depending on how you are inclined) as all's fair in love and war!

Bagsy not

You can 'bagsy not' to do something. For example "Bagsy not taking out the rubbish!" If there are more than two people liable to take out the rubbish then all the others will then have to race not to be last to say 'bagsy not'. The last person to say 'bagsy not' has to do the undesirable task.

On the ball

To be on the ball is to be aware of your situation, to be receptive and responsive to events, e.g. When the tap started gushing water, Gareth was on the ball and instantly ran to the stop cock valve.

I suppose it comes from the idea that when you're on the ball in a sporting sense you have to keep your wits about you, as at that moment all the action is focussed on you.

Balls of steel

This expression has its roots in the idea that to be brave, you have to have balls (i.e. testicles). The bigger the balls, the braver you are – a very macho idea. Therefore to have balls of steel means you're unquestionably brave and can get through even the scariest of moments. Particularly big **bluffs** require you to suppress all doubt and fear. Someone who can carry this off, a big bluff, is often said to have balls of steel. The phrase is seldom applied to female bravery for obvious reasons.

Banter

Banter in a literal sense is a tongue-in-cheek to-and-fro conversation. In a more general sense, banter can describe the type of humour that is typical of your social interactions:

"Well, sorry if the banter's not to your taste!"
(literally: our type of talk and humour doesn't suit you)

"What's this banter?"
(literally: what's been said? what's up?)

You might have several types of banter and maybe not aware that you move from one sort to another, e.g. serious banter for talking to a police man or silly banter when you're talking to a kid.

Beer, Beers

Although beer is literally ale or stout, 'beers' in the plural and colloquial sense, means lager.

"Dave, get the beers in!"
(literally: Dave, buy enough lager for all of us now)

Also see **get in (G²)** if you still don't understand the phrase above.

Biggles

Captain W. E. Johns' fictional pilot James Bigglesworth, affectionately called Biggles by his flying comrades, is well known for his 'Boys' Own'* style adventures. His iconic leather flying goggles and British stiff upper lip have stereotyped the early twentieth century gentleman flyer.

See the game 'Bunnies' (p117) for the variation 'Captain Bigglesworth' to find out how this fictional character ended up in *The Lash*.

*'Boys' Own Paper', which ran from 1879 to 1967, was a British story paper aimed at boys. It contained adventure stories and articles which have in recent times been critiqued as right wing and imperialistic.

Biplane

A biplane is a fixed-wing aircraft with two double wings. It is the plane design used in the early years of aviation. See **Sopwith Camel (S)** for a First World War example of a biplane.

Bite your lip

This figurative and sometimes literal expression means to hold back from saying something – usually because it will be of no help or will land you in trouble. Sometimes in life you have to bite your lip even if you think you know better. You may also have to bite your lip if the moment for you to talk has passed.

e.g. The mechanic was talking **bollocks** but Chris bit his lip until he had finished before telling him his hobby is restoring cars.

Black Hawk Down

A 2001 film by Ridley Scott based on the events of the Battle of Mogadishu in 1993.

Blessing sign

This is the sign that you see the Pope do over people's heads. Prophets and saints are also frequently pictured making this sign. To make the sign the index finger and middle finger are held up and the other fingers and thumb are tucked away. This sign is made with both hands in 'I'm Colonel Puff' (see p141) at the Puff Puff stage to double-tap the table.

The blessign sign is the same as when you tap twice in I'm Colonel Puff (p141)

Bluff, Bluffs, Bluffing

To bluff is to pretend to have or not to have something in order to deceive your opponent.

Double bluff

In a double bluff you try to look like you're **bluffing**, even though you're not, in the hope that you can fool your opponent into thinking you're bluffing and making a wrong call. Sound confusing? That's because I suppose it is meant to. A double bluff is a more complex mind game than a bluff. Usually (but not always) you will need a bluff to set a precedent before a double bluff can be attempted.

Bollocks

(for another useful swear word see **fuck**)
Bollocks can mean 'that's not true', i.e. lies. Furthermore it can be used to express shock, distress or dissatisfaction, whilst all along also being a word for testicles.

The bomb

This is when something is **great**, the best. It describes the idea of something making a big impact, as I'm sure an explosion would.

"That film was the bomb!"

To drop the bomb

This can mean to poo or fart but I use it to mean making a big impact, to blow up on the scene creating excitement and shock.

e.g. As the DJ drops a great **tune**, Nate exclaims, "Boom! He's just dropped the bomb!"

The expression can also mean delivering particularly bad news to someone.

e.g. "I'm going to have to drop the bomb on Will. I'm going to tell him I slept with his girlfriend last night."

Boss

(a.k.a. the **Administrator**)
The Boss is the ultimate **law**. To boss something (or 'boss it') is to exercise complete control over a situation. Every decision the Boss makes is final and must be acted upon instantly. To be a good Boss you must be fair and be an expert on your subject, i.e. the drinking game you are playing.

You will never be universally loved as the boss of a game, especially if players are reluctant to take fines. In which case you will be required to be a **cunt** or **asshole**.

Brainiac

A colloquial term for someone intelligent.

A buff

A buff is a serious fan. The word is usually used to describe someone with a specific area of expertise.

Buffalo, Buffaloed

This is left-hand drinking only. If anyone picks up their drink with their right hand, **call**[4] "Buffalo!" Right-hand drinking is punished with a fine, usually finishing off the drink they drank with their right hand.

Bumpers

When you go bowling (see 'Drink Bowling' on p159) you can play with bumpers. These are foam fillers or bars that go in the gutter (the drain either side of the alley) to ensure that you don't get a 'no score'. Bumpers are only used by children and **lame** players.

Bunder, Bundered, Bundering

(a.k.a. **chunder**)

1. This is to be sick, often in a violent way and usually induced by excessive drinking.

e.g. "Steve has just bundered everywhere!" or "I bundered after **downing** the punishment last night."

2. A tactical bunder is making yourself sick, usually by sticking your fingers down your throat. This is done in order to sober up (usually in the deluded hope you'll **pull**) or to keep drinking. Tacticals are usually employed during big **sessions** of drinking when you simply can't take any more and have to clear some space.

There is no shame in having a tactical as long as it really was a tactical. Some people claim to have pulled a tactical when they have been involuntarily sick from drink. A tactical shows that you treat the **lash** like an art form. Knowing when to pull a tactical is a difficult decision. It is also quite a 'sick' idea and usually undertaken by only the most **hardcore** of drinkers.

e.g. "I pulled a tactical earlier." or "Sorry I'm late, just had a little tactical before the lash begins!"

All business is finished, Is all business finished?

In certain drinking games all action for a given round[2] must be complete before the game moves on. As the **Administrator**, you must ensure that every player has ample chance to take part in the game. It is courteous to check that all players have done everything they intended to do by saying, "Is all business finished?" or "Are we all done?" With this statement you are making it clear that the round has concluded.

Butler

The Butler is someone who provides table service and generally aids the smooth running of the game but does not actually play. Usually they fulfil this role as the **Administrator** when player numbers are high. To be the Butler is a privilege. When the role is imposed as a punishment it is known as the **Gopher**.

The Butler distributes the drinks.

C
Call, Calls, Calling, Called
1. This sort of call is a vocal or physical action. The person doing the action or saying the specific word or phrase is the caller. In 'Slammers, Sliders, Spiders' (p103) the presenting team perform the 'Slammer', 'Slider' and 'Spider' actions. They are 'doing the calls'. In 'Yee-ha!' (p53) saying and doing a 'Hoedown' is also a call.

2. In this sense, making a call is offering a guess or gambit. The caller is the person making the guess.

Here's an example from 'Spoof' (p21).

Player 2: "I call five." Player 2 is making a guess. He or she is the caller.

3. Simply to say or ask for something.

4. To call in this sense is to point out somebody's behaviour to other players and in particular the **Administrator** of the game. The behaviour highlighted is usually a misdemeanour.

During a game played with **International Drinking Rules (I)**, Player 5 notices Player 9 has pointed and brings it to the attention of the Administrator:

Player 5: "No pointing, Player 9!"

5. You can also be called to drink by the Administrator if you have transgressed. This is an order to drink!

e.g. The Administrator: "Drink, Player 9!"

6. This type of call is a direct challenge. When you are called in this sense there are usually **stakes** involved and you are being asked to prove yourself by one or more players. This sort of call comes from **poker** where you have to match another player's bet in order to see their cards.

If someone calls you then they will usually have had to risk something in order to challenge you. In a drinking game this is usually a bigger drinking fine.

This sort of calling is fundamental to 'Pyramid Cheat' (p171).

Player 3: "I have two nines. Player 8, drink the fines."

Player 4: "I'm going to call you cheat. You haven't got two nines, Player 3!"

7. 'Called' = known as

8. A decision, usually one that is difficult to make.

e.g. "Make the call! Are you going to turn left or right?"

Jimmy Carr
An English-Irish comedian, famed for his deadpan style and dark sense of humour.

Casualty
Drinking games often take their terminology from the language of war. Anyone who can no longer drink (or has gone **man down (M)**) is said to be a casualty.

Chat

1. Chat is your verbal skills. To have chat is to have the gift of the gab.

e.g. "My mate Gav has loads of chat."

Chat is not always informed but is always carried off with confidence and charisma.

The opposite of chat is 'no chat'. Someone with no chat is uninspiring and unremarkable, doesn't talk at all or is very boring with what they say.

2. A chat can be a discussion of a serious nature. If someone asks for a chat with you, they actually want a frank discussion with you.

e.g. After Tanya had lost the company £10 million on the stock market, her boss asks her, "Can we have a little chat in my office?"

3. Backchat is addressing an authority figure in an unsuitable way. A teacher might say to a student "For that backchat, you'll be seeing me in detention at lunch time!"

Backchat is always satisfying for the person doing it but is invariably ill-received and will often land you in more trouble. The most unacceptable place for backchat is in the military. It will not get you anywhere if you express your opinion to a Drill Sergeant!

Drinking **sessions** can take on military qualities. The **Boss** or **Administrator** should never except backchat.

Check out

1. The expression 'check out' comes from the world of darts. The check out is the throw which gives the player their final target score, usually by hitting a double.

I use check out when a player exits a drinking game by following a specific routine. To check out in 'Fives' (p31) players must finish with an exit statement such as "Thank you very much, ladies and gentlemen, for a lovely game of 'Fives'".

2. Check out also means 'regard', 'pay heed', 'look at' or 'look here'.

e.g. Pulling a stunt on her bike, Kate exclaims, "Check this out!"

Chequered past

To have a chequered past is to have a few skeletons in the closet. I do love the way when you're explaining an English saying often another saying says it best!

If you have a chequered past it means that you may have done things that do not reflect well on your present self. The relevant acts are usually performed in the naivety of youth and with hindsight seem socially unpalatable.

Chin, Chinning, Chinned

Literally, drinking your drink **in one (O)** attempt. The expression refers to the fact that in the process of drinking you tilt your head back, exposing your chin and also to the fact that drink spillages and your glass come into contact with your chin. A common expression is "Chin it!" and in university circles people are heard to say, "Chin it, **fresher!**"

The double-handed technique — elbows wide
and then chin it!

Chinook

The Boeing CH-47 Chinook is an iconic heavy-lift helicopter with two rotors. It is used by the British military (amongst others) for troop movement, artillery emplacement and battlefield re-supply.

Chunder, Chundered, Chundering
(a.k.a. **bunder**)

A word for being sick, in particular if the sick is lumpy. A chunder is usually brought on by excessive drinking. The term 'chunder' is a term used less frequently in drinking circles than the word bunder.

e.g. "I chundered." or "Have you just chundered?"

Circle go games

Many drinking games follow patterns and thus can be categorised into groups. The circle **go** game type is one of the most popular, and in this book I have ring fenced these games into their own chapter.

A circle go game is characterised by sitting in a circle and having a go – no surprise there then! They often have actions or words to send the go on in a specific direction. As a general rule the game usually moves to the left, however this is not always true. Skilful play will ensure you drink less in these types of games.

'Yee-ha!' (p53) is the perfect example of a circle go game

Cirrhosis of the liver

One of the causes of cirrhosis is chronic alcoholism. Medically speaking, cirrhosis of the liver is a condition in which scar tissue replaces normal healthy tissue. The scar tissue restricts blood flow to the organ and prevents it from functioning normally.

For more information on cirrhosis of the liver and the dangers of drink **check out (C²)** *www.britishlivertrust.org.uk* and *www.drinkaware.co.uk*

Even *The Lash* understands that drinking isn't great for your health – please take care!

Class

To have class is to exhibit facets of etiquette and style of a high social order. However, this word has also come to mean being well-mannered and having respect for oneself in all aspects of life, not just in terms of appearance.

Claw

When a hand is wrapped around a pint glass, the four fingers of the hand take on a claw shape. A claw is a unit of fine equal to the amount of liquid covered by the four fingers. This is approximately half a pint in a standard pint glass, though the amount depends on the width of your **fingers** and the shape of the glass.

A claw is basically four fingers of drink

Clock drinking

When you are clock drinking you may only drink with your left or right hand, depending on the position of the minute arm on an analogue clock. Between the hour and half past (when the minute hand is on the right side of the clock face) it's right-hand drinking only, and between half past and the hour (when the minute hand is on the left side of the clock face) it's left-hand drinking only.

Coaching

Coaching is when a player or the **Administrator** teaches another player how to play the game. The Administrator should perform some preliminary coaching at the start of all games to ensure everyone has a basic understanding of how the game proceeds.

Player 2 is being taught 'Fives' (p31)

No coaching

Sometimes you will impose a 'no coaching' rule. A player having difficulties understanding the game must not be aided or instructed but left alone to wonder where and why they are going wrong. The 'no coaching' call is particularly useful in 'Animal Kingdom' (p130) and 'I'm Colonel Puff' (p141). The **Administrator** can offer help but only if the player's struggle seems endless. If any player other than the Administrator aids the participant in question, they should be fined heavily for breaking the 'no coaching' rule. This always applies when **clock drinking (C)** is in effect. Anyone caught drinking with the wrong hand is fined. No coaching is alsoa facet of **no mercy rules (M)**.

Player 7 is reprimanded for teaching Player 1!

Cocky

If someone is cocky, they are cocksure; they have an inflated, sense of self-worth often tinged with arrogance and sometimes recklessness. Cocky, I'm sure, has some grounding in the self-important swagger of a male chicken (a cock) in the hen house.

The phrase 'a cocky look' as I use it in *The Lash* means an arrogant, I've-got-one-over-on-you' type of look. It is likely to pass over a player's face if they think they've escaped punishment.

Comedown

The low experience after the euphoria of a drugs trip. This applies to drink as well (drink is a drug!) though we usually (euphemistically) **call**[7] it the Monday blues or such like. I refer to it as a **trough**.

Cunt, Cunted, Cuntish

This is an awful word and to be a cunt is the worst state a human can possibly achieve: evil, selfish, amoral. To be 'cuntish' is to act in an abhorrent antagonistic manner.

e.g. "Stop being so cuntish!"

Sometimes in a drinking game you may have to be a bit cuntish if someone tries to refuse to take a fine. You have to think as the **Administrator** not as an individual player. The player must be forced to take the fine in the name of fairness. If you have been a good Administrator you will have outlined all the fines to be expected at the start of the game so no player can say "But I didn't know!" If they are playing the game they have accepted the consequences and you have every right to be a cunt to them if they refuse. The reality of a drinking game is you drink and you cannot have the fun without the forfeit. As the cunt, you are forced to make them see this reality!

e.g. The Administrator forces a reluctant Player 1 to drink their fine. "Look I know it's hard, but I've got to be cuntish. It's for your own good!" Player 1 replies, "You're a right cunt!"

D
Dance-off

Where two people or two groups of people battle against each other using dance moves to decide who is better. They take it in turns to make attacks and reposts until one side admits the other is superior. The decision is reached by communal agreement as to who was the best, even if it means an opponent admitting their competitor was better. If the dance-off is truly competitive, and not governed by the 'rules of the street' (where it is good manners to accept defeat from a more worthy opponent), then neutral observers vote to decide a winner.

Debauchery, Debauched
When things go a bit wrong after a large quantity of drink. Often characterised by nakedness, bodily fluids being drunk and general debasing and decivilizing of oneself and the whole situation.

Jack Dee
Jack Dee is best known as a stand-up comedian. He is a master of dead-pan humour.

Depth charge
This is when someone drops a shot glass full of **spirits** (also see **shorts**) into a larger glass containing drink such as **beer**, cider etc.

The pint has been depth charged with a shot

Des.

Short for designated driver. There's one rule that must be adhered to if Des. is **out**² and that is "Des. doesn't pay!" Why? Because they have to put up with all your crap drunk **chat**¹ so you need to **shout** them some **soft** drinks and pay their entry if you go to a club.

Treat your des. well, after all they are your taxi!

Dirty pint

A dirty 'pint' does not always equal a pint in quantity; it is a generic term for a mixed drink. A dirty pint is a description of any drink that has had many drinks added to it which has made it turn an unusual colour. Often it is pretty horrible to drink and more alcoholic. The usual thing to do is to add **spirits** to a quantity of lager or cider. A dirty pint creation is an art form and I've seen **Twiglets**™ and in extreme cases, ashtray contents and phlegm added. This is not meant to be nice! Ironically it is usually given as a birthday treat and has involved a **whip round** (W) to get the money to buy it. Due to the fact that all of their so-called friends have paid for the dirty pint, the birthday boy or girl feels obliged to drink it. This in itself is **peer pressure**, but if the birthday boy or girl is still reluctant, some of the songs described under peer pressure are used to ensure it is all drunk. A large quantity of dirty pint is made by combining drinks in a communal vessel, as in 'Arrogance' (p26) and 'The Challenge' (p16).

Dominate, Dominates, Domination, Dominating

To exert an undeniable force over something or someone. If you dominate something, your greater power (knowledge or strength) allows you bend it to your will. If you dominate a drinking game, you know every facet of the game inside and out. Mastering the game will allow you to control the social situation surrounding the game and prevent it turning into an **Irish Parliament (I)**.

The done thing, not the done thing
The done thing is the socially acceptable way to do something. If you are told you have done something which is 'not the done thing', you have made a **faux pas (F)**.

e.g. "Using that spoon is not the done thing, this is the fish course!"

This expression has gone out of fashion. It is now seen as archaic and extremely upper class – the sort of language that Captain **Biggles** would have come out with, followed by "Be a good chap!" and "Spiffing!"

Double a double
In many drinking games the direction of play reverses when a word is said twice or an action is done twice. It is usually forbidden for a player who has had the **go** reversed to them to then send it back the way it came. This practice is called doubling a double. It can lead to battles where players **hog** the go by sending it back and forth between themselves. If doubling a double is forbidden by the rules of the game, then as the **Administrator** you should ensure that everyone appreciates this before play commences. If anyone does double a double, you should say "You can't double a double!" and fine the player who did the second double.

Double or bust
A double or bust situation is when a losing player is allowed back into a game by upping (usually doubling) the **stakes**. It can also mean to have another chance, but with a higher risk involved if you lose again. Often a player's inability to prevent themselves from admitting defeat after the first loss can lead to an even greater loss, i.e. bust.

Where I've used this phrase it means to double the drinking fine whilst giving a player one more chance. It's not always their last chance, as they might have to double up again because of an **auto re-challenge**.

If one player calls another a 'cheat' in 'Pyramid Cheat' (p171) this is a straight double or bust situation. The challenger can win double if they are correct and their opponent will be required to drink double the fine, but they may also hit bust, if they are wrong in their assumptions.

Double parked, Double parking

When someone has more than one drink in front of them, this is referred to as being double parked. The oldest drink or drinks must be **downed** or **chinned** until the player is single parked again. You can of course be triple or quadruple parked (or worse), which will mean you have to drink a considerable amount in order to satisfy parking regulations (see **International Drinking Rules (I)**).

Down, Downs, Downed, Downing

To down a drink is to finish it **in one (O)** go, just like **chinning**. I suppose the origin of this colloquialism comes from the fact you're pouring liquid 'down' into your body.

Drink-off

A drink-off is a quick drinking competition. The word drink-off is a bastardisation of **dance-off**. Two or more people race to be the first to finish their drink. The winner goes **out[1]** while the losers play on.

1, 2, 3... go! A simple race to finish drinks in a drink-off

E

E.T.

'E.T.' stands for 'etiquette tap'. This is the action of tapping either yourself on the chest or another player's glass or vessel when you have finished your drink. It is a sort of social grace marking the point at which you finished your drink. An E.T. is most frequently used by someone who has just drunk a large quantity of drink, in which situation they are using the action to say, "Look I've done it."

Someone who says, "I've E.T.ed **out**[1]," means they have finished their drink and marked this point with a tap.

If someone says to you, "You didn't E.T.!" you may have committed a **faux pas (F)**. If you do not E.T. sometimes it can mean a repeat fine. If you are playing the E.T. rule you must, in your capacity as **Administrator** make it clear at the start of play. E.T.ing can become a **game of life (G)** for some **veterans** of drinking games. See 'Next!' (p9) for an example of a game where E.T.s are part of the rules.

E.T. on your chest

E.T. to another player

Everything wet must go!
A **great (G)** drinking saying which basically means "Finish all the drinks!" We live in a world of scarce resources and I therefore find it a heinous crime that when a big **session** finishes with the taxi or the lift arriving outside, people just get up and leave half-filled drinks strewn about. To prevent this, **call**[3] "Everything wet must go!" and then have a mad two minutes Hoovering (maybe that should now be called Dysoning) drinks down your throat. They say many hands make light work, as indeed do mouths when it comes to drinking.

Extreme see **Hardcore** or **Medieval**

F

F-14 Tomcat

The Grumman F-14 Tomcat, two-seater, supersonic fighter came to popular attention after it appeared in the 1980s film **Top Gun (T)**. The US Navy took the F-14 out of service in 2006 but ironically it is still used today by the Air Force of the Islamic Republic of Iran.

Faint-hearted

The origin of the saying is people, and women in particular, fainting in the event of something shocking or gruesome happening. Your heart is traditionally the place you get courage from, so to be faint-hearted is to have no courage or fortitude. *The Lash* is not for the faint-hearted!

Faux pas

A social blunder usually stemming from an error of etiquette.

Festive

(a.k.a. **merry**)
Heartily drunk, just like you get at Christmas, hence the term.

Flagship

This is an example to be followed, i.e. an archetype. The saying comes from the Navy where every fleet has a flagship. This was usually the best ship, and all other ships tried to emulate its example.

In terms of drinking games, a flagship game is an original. It may have spawned rules which were then copied and used in other games.

In my opinion there are two flagship games in *The Lash*: '21s' (p82) and 'Yee-ha!' (p53). Once you're familiar with these games you'll notice that similar rules appear in many other games.

Finger, Fingers

A standard unit for fines, measured by the width of one finger on a standard pint glass, or any other type of glass if you're not a stickler for the rules. Eight fingers usually equals one pint, though this depends on hand size. Fingers are a great way to fine as it takes into account the relative body size of the players – a big person is likely to be able to handle more drink than a small person with smaller hands. See next page.

A finger of drink — the level under the finger

Bruce Forsyth

British game show host Brucey is a national **legend**! He was the card master in the ITV game show *Play your Cards Right*, a game similar to 'Pyramid' (p168), especially in its presentation. If you manage to emulate Bruce's charisma and easy manner in your role as the Card Master, you'll be the king of all **banter**.

Fresher

A student in their first year at university. This is often used as a derogatory term at universities, either towards an actual fresher or someone who seems to have less experience than yourself.

Frown upon, Frowned upon

To look upon something or someone disapprovingly, especially when a **faux pas (F)** has been committed, or someone has done something that is 'not cricket'. In drinking games, cheating and not accepting fines are frowned upon.

Stephen Fry

An English comedian, writer, actor, humorist, novelist, columnist, film maker and television personality. He is famous for his sharp wit and intellectual **banter**.

Fuck, Fucked, Fucking, Fuck-up

One of the most versatile words in the English language. It primarily means 'to have sexual intercourse with' but it has many uses. For a very funny explanation of the multi-functional nature of this word, search for 'Using Proper English: The F Word' on YouTube.

1. 'Fuck' is usually added to a sentence in order to add emphasis.

2. If you are fucked, it means you are in a disadvantageous position. The situation is usually, though not always, irretrievable. When you are fucked you often leave yourself open to **domination** (or a **fucking**[1]).

e.g. After crashing his girlfriend's new car, Ken knew he was fucked.

3. 'Fuck-up' is a crude way of saying mistake (also see **mess up (M)**)

e.g. "Well, that was a fuck-up."

A fuck-up can also be a person who has made a mistake. In a game they are known as the fuck-up until another player transgresses and take on the title.

In a drinking game it is not uncommon for the player to the left of whoever has made an error to restart the game.

e.g. "Left of the fuck-up starts!"

In drinking games the fuck-up does not restart because restarting is sometimes a privilege or advantageous. It is only when restarting is difficult, as in 'Gloucester Directions' (p97) that the fuck-up will be asked to restart. In this case restarting is a punishment.

G

Game of life

When the rules of a drinking game have invaded your day-to-day behaviour it has become a 'game of life'. People like me are sad enough to include the rules of drinking games in their everyday life. I know people who say 'the number before 22' rather than say the unmention-able '21' (see '21' p82). See **unmentionable words (U)** for more information on this drinking game phenomenon.

Gay

This used to mean happy, but now means homosexual. Furthermore, the word in recent times has transformed again to mean 'not good', 'silly', 'stupid', 'not cool' or 'shit'. The term has not escaped its negative origins as heterosexual derision of homosexuals.

e.g. Someone half-heartedly threatens to drop something you own into a pond. Your say, "Come on, don't be gay!"

Something is not too cool. You say, "It's a bit gay, isn't it?"

Geo-socio situation

An erudite way of saying geographical and social situation. Drinking games have a wide appeal to all areas and social groups of the UK. Maybe you're **Indie**, **Urban** or a **Jock** or maybe you consider yourself pretty mainstream. Whatever and whoever you are, you can take a drinking game and change it to suit you friendship group.

Get

1. To 'get something' is to understand or comprehend.

e.g. Instructor: "I hope you got that?"
Mike: "I get it. Don't worry, that briefing covered it all."

2. To 'get the drinks in' is to buy or fetch drinks for the group. This is usually a **round**[1] of drinks.

e.g. "Gaz, get the **beers** in!"

3. 'Get this' means 'listen to this', i.e. understand or receive this information. It is most frequently used before saying something shocking or controversial.

4. The destination you seek is drunkenness so to be 'getting there' is to be on your way to achieving this state, i.e. almost drunk.

e.g. Player 1: "Are you drunk?", Player 2: "I'm getting there!"

Play God, Playing God, God's eye

When explaining a game in *The Lash*, I have used this term to describe the viewpoint I am offering you as the reader. For tutorial reasons *The Lash* often puts you in an omnipotent position so you can understand the game better, e.g. when I show you the suit and numbers of all cards in a game.

When applied to the **Administrator** the phrase means that during a game you must have all the answers so you appear omnipotent. If you have achieved a competent understanding of the game you are administering, you can both smite the evil with fines, and, in your infinite mercy, give life to those less fortunate. With power comes responsibility, so beware!

INFO+ For more on the power of the Administrator see **Boss**.

Go

The word 'go' is used more often in this book than any other explanatory word. A go is a turn, i.e. the point in the game that you have to do something, or have the **power**.

In many drinking games, the order of the go is deliberately confusing with the result that players take their go out of turn or hesitate. When this happens the player who mistakenly thought it was their go or didn't realise it was their go, is fined for the infraction.

Gopher

A dogsbody. Someone who does the ferrying and pouring of drinks, and within reason, tends to the needs of players. Unlike the **Butler**, who is treated with respect, a Gopher is a player who is forced to take on the role as a punishment. The Gopher could be singled out by the **Administrator** because of a blunder they make in a game or because they don't understand the concept of the game and are holding the other players up. Or maybe they are continually **messing up (M)** due to the fact they are so **pissed**.

The Gopher is there to be abused by all: he or she is a slave, a jester, there to do whatever you would have him or her do for you. The Administrator should take charge if the Gopher's antics and the requests of the players start interfering with the running of the game.

A great

If something or someone is 'a great' it is not just really good, it has taken on **legendary** proportions. The expression comes from the tradition of calling rulers 'great' e.g. Alfred the Great, Alexander the Great and Catherine the Great.

H

Half-struck, Half-cut
If the clock has struck it means you're drunk, so half-struck means you're tipsy. To be cut (which can also mean having a toned muscular body) is to be drunk, so to be half-cut also means to be tipsy. See also **on your way (O)** and **getting there (G⁴)**, which have similar meanings.

Hardcore
Something or someone hardcore is extreme, the antithesis of **soft**. The most frequent use of hardcore is to describe 'hardcore porn', pornography that bares all and is highly explicit. 'Hardcore' is often used in extreme sports to describe something that is difficult and/or dangerous. I use 'hardcore' to describe extreme **lash**. Also see **savage**.

'The hardcore' in a social group are the extremists (not in the terrorist sense!) – people who take whatever they do to the extremes, for example by being hardcore drinkers. A hardcore can also mean an elite that it is difficult to join.

Head tap
Someone who has a head tap is a bit mental. Not in the cool sense of not being easily scared but in quite a scary way. Someone who has a head tap will easily fly off the handle, or may even be a psycho.

e.g. "Riley has a head tap and will probably kill someone when he goes into the army."

Someone who is less of a mental case can still have a head tap when it comes to a particular subject or activity.

e.g. "Dave's sound, but he's got a head tap when it comes to climbing."

Health and safety
The Health and Safety at Work Act 1974 is a crucial piece of legislation from the British government which ensures that employers provide their staff with a safe environment in which to work.

Unfortunately, certain people use it as an excuse to stifle non-dangerous fun. 'Health and safety' has become a by-word for over-the-top measures that make people's lives more difficult and prevent people from doing the things they want. Often some of the things that health and safety regulations cover are not practically dangerous and some would argue that health and safety is a tool of the nanny culture we experience here in Britain. We're told "You can't do this...", "You can't do that..." and often the reason given is 'health and safety'.

e.g. You might hear someone exclaim: "This is health and safety gone mad!"

You could also experience the following situation:

Officious person: "Please don't climb that!"
You: "Why not?"
Officious person: "It's health and safety!"

Hear me now
An **Ali G (A)** expression that means 'listen up' or 'listen to me'. In the 'Ali G Roman numeral' version of '21' (p82) it means X or 10 (see also **Roman numerals (R)**).

Heavy
A slang word over-used by surfers, e.g. "Oh dude, that was heavy!" which literally translates as "My friend, that was very exciting and scary." The word as it is used in *The Lash*, means serious, weighty and severe **lash**.

e.g. "That was a heavy **session** last night," or "That was some heavy lash!"

Hell of a...
(pr. **'helluva'**)
An expression commonly used by people from South West England, especially Cornwall and Devon. The phrase emphasises an adjective or describes a noun, e.g. "That was hell of a trick," or "That was a hell of a good kebab."

Hog
To 'hog' something is not to share it, like a pig (or hog) that does not like to share its food with anyone else.

Hooray Henry
A extravagantly over-the-top posh person. A stereotype commonly applied to a male or female from an upper middle class background who has attended public school.

Male Hooray Henrys are typically called Charles (know as Charley), Henry (also known as H) and Rupert (known as Ru). The female versions are often called Camilla (Millie), Charlotte (also Charley) and Georgia (Georgie). All tend to be found on the horse riding (particularly polo), shooting and sailing social scenes.

The term Hooray Henry comes from the likelihood that if you are in their company you will hear them exclaim: "HOORAY HENRY!" when their friend Henry does something worthy of acclaim.

I

Indian file

This describes people lining up one behind the other. Apparently, the saying comes from the fact that Native Americans, or Indians, used to march one behind the other, placing their feet in the footsteps of the man in front, in order to disguise their numbers from their enemies.

Indian file — one behind another

Indie

Literally means independent from the mainstream. The word describes a subculture defined by music, fashion, behaviour and beliefs that are perceived as 'normal'. Indie culture has many of the traits of the 1960s hippie counter-culture.

International Drinking Rules (I.D.R.)

There is no such thing but some people insist that certain drinking game rules are so well known that they constitute an agreed code of behaviour.

I believe that drinking rules should be made up to suit the situation and fit in with your **banter**. Nevertheless, some of the rules that are accepted as being part of I.D.R. work well so I'll give you some examples:

1. No mentioning the D-word i.e. "drink" (see also **unmentionable words (U)**).

2. No pointing

Point with your elbow not your finger!

3. No swearing

4. Left-hand drinking only (see **buffalo**)

5. **Clock drinking (C)**

6. No **double parking (D)**

I'm sure there are many more but it's up to you to make up your own rules as you see fit.

Irish Parliament

This saying is on its way out thanks to peace and stability in Northern Ireland. It was formerly used in British military circles to describe a situation where too many people are talking at once, often with conflicting opinions. In an Irish Parliament nothing can be done as no one voice **dominates**. Never let a drinking game descend to this level. There should be one voice in a drinking game and that is yours as the **Administrator**.

Anarchy rules as the game decends into a difference of opinion

Iron fist

To 'rule with an iron fist' means to rule by force. The iron fist evokes a warrior's rule (knights and warriors wore gauntlets, or iron gloves, in battle) and methods are usually physically coercive.

To crush something with an iron fist is to eliminate dissent in a ruthlessly brutal manner. Now this sounds a bit over the top for a drinking game, but the sentiment rings true. Sometimes an **Administrator** must act to prevent an uprising against a game, especially in the initial stages when players have not yet understood the rules and are reluctant to play. As the Administrator you must act quickly and efficiently to stamp out any anti-game sentiment or flouting of the rules. Sometimes a game's success will depend on the rules being strictly adhered to and pursuing its implementation despite popular disapproval.

J
Jock

An American stereotype, describing a tall, physically fit male in his late teens or early twenties, who is well known for his athletic abilities.

In Britain 'the jocks' is a generic term for a social group whose pastimes are dominated by sport. At my school you were either classed as a jock or a skater. Jocks tend to hold conservative views and are usually followers of mainstream culture. A jock can also be used to describe a Scotsman.

Me Julie
An expression used by **Ali G (A)**. Julie is Ali's love interest. He often refers to her in his interviews on *The 11 O'clock Show* and she is a central character in the film *Ali G Indahouse*. 'Me Julie' equals V (see **Roman numerals (R)**) in the 'Ali G Roman numeral' variation of '21' (p92).

Jumbo
A 'jumbo' is the nickname given to a Boeing 747, a large passenger plane.

K
Kitty
A communal **pot** of money (which all members of a group contribute to) used to buy drinks. Its use is prevalent on **tours** and often the money is taken care of by the Tour Secretary (a position of responsibility) who hands over sums to the **Gopher** when he or she is required to buy things.

L
Lame
Describes something weak and pathetic, the antithesis of strong and **dominating**.

e.g. "That was a lame attempt."

Lancaster Bomber
The Avro Lancaster was a British Second World War bomber. It was famed as 'the Dambuster' during the 1943 Operation Chastise raids. The sound of a Lancaster starting-up is the noise you need to try and emulate if you are an engine in the **biplane** or **jumbo** in the 'Captain Bigglesworth' variation of 'Bunnies' (p124).

Lash, Lashed, Lashing

This is what this is all about! 'Lash' is the term used to describe drinking (usually heavily) that will result in you getting **pissed**. When lashing, it is the drinking that matters. Although lash is a social thing, it can appear to be anti-social as concentrating on the games is fundamental. The drinking can take on militant characteristics: failure to drink is not acceptable.

You can be said to be "On the lash." People also sometimes say, "Let's get on it," (i.e. the lash) or "Let's get some lash on."

Hard lash

This is one step down from **savage** lash but still involves drinking a sustained intoxicating amount.

Lash monster, Lash monsters

A person who excels at drinking large quantities of alcohol very fast and seemingly with no ill effects. Usually a lash monster is a rather crude or vulgar sort of person who is not fazed about getting naked or becoming **debauched**.

The Law

Drinking games are not a democratic institution. Do not argue with the law. Think about getting stopped by the police: does arguing ever help you out? No, it usually lands you in even more trouble! Drinking games are exactly the same. So if you are the **Administrator** don't accept any questioning of your authority. Anyone who answers back (see **backchat (C³)**) must be punished. You are 'The Law'. You say what is right and wrong. See also **playing God (G)**.

Lead off

If you 'lead off' a group, you show the way by going first. When you lead off in a game, you're not starting first for your own benefit but in order to help other less experienced players.

e.g. "I know most of you haven't played before but I'll lead off and we'll play a couple of practice **rounds²**."

This is *not* the same as a gun start (see 'Fives' p31).

Player 4 leads off with a 'Yee-ha!'

A legend, Legendary

It is the highest honour to be called a legend. Only when you are truly great can you hope to enter the realms of legend. If something is legendary then it is fantastic, incomparably good.

Lot

A number of persons or things regarded as a group. I use 'lot' to describe a group of fines that are administered as a single unit, like antiques grouped into lots for auction.

M

Mad drunk

(a.k.a. **pissed**)
A type of intoxicated experience that is crazed, aggressive, loud and always uncoordinated.

e.g. "Let's get mad drunk!"

Man down

If someone goes man down then they have had too much to drink which has caused semi-unconsciousness and/or vomiting (**bundering**[1] or **chundering**).

e.g. "Ben's gone man down," or "Ben's man down."

You could admit to a friend, "I'm a bit man down." This would mean you're in a bit of a **trough**, rather than actually **fucked²**.

This drinking saying comes from mimicking the army cry if a soldier is shot. You are implying that the person in question is a **casualty**.

Man up
(see **step up (S)**)
To man up is to steel yourself for action, to galvanise yourself, to face up to the challenge and to stop being afraid (a.k.a. **soft**).

e.g. Will is standing at the top of the bungee jump. His mates call, "Man up!"

You can also tell someone to man up if they're looking down.

e.g. "Come on, man up, Olly!"

Medieval
Used to describe **hardcore**, brutal and uncivilised **lash**. A description for a drinking **session** which is particular torturous and horrendous and is implemented with unsubtle militant methods, often simply **chinning** vast quantities of alcohol very quickly.

No mercy rules
This is a state of play that can be imposed by the **Administrator**. No mercy involves the creation of a totalitarian atmosphere, enforced by the Administrator.

You could impose it during a super-easy game or one that the players have had plenty of opportunity to learn. If you want to get a **lash** on, no mercy rules up the anti and make the **session** militant.

No mercy rules are essentially the creation of a pressurised situation where there is no such thing as an excuse! Do *not* help any players understand the game. Players can't ask "Why did I go wrong?" and if they **fuck up³** they simply have to drink and work out where they went wrong for themselves.

During no mercy play any **back chat (C³)** must be severely punished!

Fines must be taken in their entirety and you yield nothing to the players. Under these conditions they deserve everything they get *and more*! This is when the Administrator of the game is at his most **cuntish**!

No mercy rules go hand in hand with the **no coaching (C²)** rule. You can play no coaching without no mercy at a more relaxed drinking session, but you *can't* play no mercy without the no coaching rule.

Merry
(a.k.a. **festive**)
Literally meaning tipsy on drink (or **pissed**). This word may come from the sense of festive merriment. When you get merry on alcohol at Christmas the merriness is often accompanied by rosy cheeks.

Half-struck/Half-cut (H) mean pretty much the same thing as merry but are used in different social situations:

Merry usually said to family or close friends. Half-struck is more formal, could be used at a works-do or reception. Half-cut is cruder than half-struck, one to use when you're **out²** with your friends, usually not said to a family member or social superior.

Mess up, Messed up, Messes up
To mess up is to go wrong. It is to make a mistake in respect of the rules of the particular drinking game being played.

Messy
If something gets messy it goes beyond the usual limits and in so doing, creates destruction, i.e. mess. In terms of **lash** if a **session** gets messy it loses all order and restraint. This means the session becomes **savage** or **hardcore** and **debauchery** may ensue.

e.g. Gemma brings two litres of vodka to the **pre-lash (P)** and exclaims, "This drinking **session** is about to get messy!"

Mine sweeping
A technique not to be encouraged (see **drink spiked (S)**) but frequently employed by the cheapskate student. In busy bars and clubs, people who are drunk often forget about their drinks and to mine sweep is to

actively seek 'undefended' drinks in order to steal them (I would rather say borrow their contents!) This is free ambrosia to the hard-up student.

Just be careful you're not caught as you could either be accused of drink spiking or if you're unlucky enough to be caught swiping some **ruffneck's** drink, then you'll be beaten within an inch of your life.

The mix
The mix is literally the drink made from mixing drinks together (a concoction) in a central communal vessel (a.k.a. the **pot**). If the drink formed is particularly horrendous, i.e. strong or distasteful, then the mix is know as a **dirty pint (D)**.

e.g. Jen hovered her Bacardi over the communal drinking vessel which already contained what looked like an evil concoction and was told by all, "Get it in the mix!"

Move off, Moves off
To move off is army slang for relocating from one place to another.

e.g. "We'll move off from delta point at 0800 hours."

I have used the phrase in *The Lash* in the sense of the **go** passing in a certain direction.

N
Has your name on it
If something has your name on it, it has been allocated to you. Often the thing that has your name on is not something you want. In the context of *The Lash,* the **Administrator** might say:

"Because of that mistake John, this fine has your name on it!"

N.F.I.
A **T.L.A.** (three letter abbreviation), meaning 'not **fucking**[1] interested'. I hate this expression but it is often used when someone who is being fined gives **back chat (C³)** to the **Boss** or **Administrator** of a game. If the Administrator is a particular tyrant or **cunt** they might turn to the guilty party and simply say "N.F.I. mate… **chin** it!"

Nigh-on, Well-nigh

Nigh literally means 'near'. 'Well-nigh' and 'nigh-on' are used to mean 'almost' or 'pretty much'.

e.g. "That exam was nigh-on impossible," or "That exam was well-nigh impossible".

On the nose

(see **spot on**)

This is a horse racing expression. If you bet on the nose you are betting that a particular horse will come in first (as opposed to an each way bet, when you bet on a horse to come first or second). I use this expression to describe betting that a certain event will happen. The bet is only right if you get it *exactly* right; there can be no grey areas with an on-the-nose bet, only black and white, right or wrong. It's no good coming second, for there is no prize for second place.

Nothing matters more than the game

This is the subtitle to *The Lash* because it is a great saying for the **Administrator** to bring out if players are not giving their full attention to the game.

The Administrator: "**Chin** it, Player 2!"
Player 2: "But my phone rang!"
The Administrator: "Nothing matters more than the game!"

O

Opening

The phrase 'to leave an opening' is used to describe a situation in competitive circumstances when one player has the opportunity to win but fails to take it, thus giving their opponent a chance to punish their mistake. A player is said to have figuratively left an opening through which their competitor has come, i.e. this player didn't shut the other player out of the game by winning at the first opportunity.

In one

To **down** in one is to drink all of your drink at the first attempt (see **chin**).

e.g. "Down in one, **fresher**!'

On your way
(see **pissed**)
If you're on your way, you've passed tipsy (or **half-struck/half-cut (H)**) and you're **getting there (G⁴)**. You're on your way to your destination, a state of drunkenness.

Out
1. To 'go out' means to leave a situation and not be part of it anymore. Sometimes going out of a game is a good thing, at other times it can mean you are the loser. It all depends on the rules and set up of the game.

e.g. "Jim dropped out of the game."

2. To 'be out' means to be out and about, i.e. not at home but socialising.

e.g. "Are you out tonight?"

3. The expression 'to out' is an extension of 'outing' someone as homosexual. It means to reveal someone's secrets without their consent. If it happens to you then you have been 'outed'.

4. An outing, as in a team outing, is an organised – or more likely disorganised – excursion to do something out of the ordinary (though you can also have an outing to do something mundane). An outing can also be referred to as a **tour**, although strictly speaking a tour is more of a holiday away and an outing a day trip.

e.g. "The girls went on an outing to Blackpool"

5. Out of line was originally a military term. Being out of line meant being out of your place in the parade or battle line. You would often receive a severe punishment if you were found to be out of line. Nowadays the term is more commonly used in the civilian world if you've done something wrong, against the rules, socially unacceptable or even shocking.

e.g. "Why did you hit that guy? You're out of line!"

P

Paper, scissors, stone

(a.k.a. rock, paper, scissors)
A game using hand signals to represent paper, scissors and a stone. On a count of three, two players hold out their hands. One hand signal always beats another. If both players show the same signal, then it's repeated. You win by scoring 'best of three'.

Paper – hand held out flat
- paper beats stone. The paper 'suffocates' the stone. I never really understood stood the logic behind this suffocation
- paper loses to scissors.

Scissors – first and middle fingers held out, tips towards your opponent
- scissors beat paper. Scissors 'cut' the paper
- scissors lose to stone.

Stone – hand held out in a fist
- stone beats scissors. The stone 'blunts' the scissors
- stone loses to paper.

The game is often used to decide who does something undesirable. The game always concludes with a loser who will have to do the undesirable task. This is usually a two player game although it is possible to play with more in a championship set-up.

The game 'Fives' (p31) can be used in a similar way, and I believe makes 'scissors, paper, stone' redundant.

Scissors

Paper

Stone

Parkinson's disease

First of all, I want to apologize for my use of this terrible disease in this book. Parkinson's is an awful affliction, which strikes with impunity. However it was very useful for describing shaking of an uncontrolled type, which is required when creating an engine in the 'Captain Bigglesworth' variation of 'Bunnies' (p117).

Parkinson's disease is a degenerative disorder affecting the central nervous system. The most visible symptom of Parkinson's disease is muscle tremor, which makes the sufferer shake uncontrollably. Famous sufferers are boxing **legend** Muhammad Ali and actor Michael J Fox.

Parcour

This sport or pastime or parcour was founded by David Belle in France. Parcour is also known as free running, and in recent times has received much media attention, for example in the television show *Jump London* and the 2006 James Bond film *Casino Royale*. The principle of parcour is to move as quickly and efficiently as possible from one point to another using the agility of the human body. It is usually practised in **urban** areas and has encouraged people to look differently at the built environment.

Paid, Paying to see someone's cards

This expression comes from the world of **poker**. In poker when a player matches a bet they can ask to see what cards the other player has in his or her hand.

I use the term to describe times when a player risks a fine in order to challenge another player in the context of the game. Paying to see someone's cards with drink is fundamental to 'Pyramid Cheat' (p171).

Peer pressure

This is social pressure exerted in order to ensure that a reluctant player pays the fine they have incurred. Peer pressure uses the fear of social exclusion to motivate an individual to perform their punishment. Once the punishment is completed they are congratulated and feel the warmth of inclusion.

Here are some songs that that you can use to exercise peer pressure and encourage individuals to drink, or all these songs can be heard on the website at *www.thelash.eu* under the tab 'songs'.

The Captain of the Ship
Nick is the captain of the ship,
Of our ship,
Nick is the captain of the ship,
Of our ship,
So let's drop the anchor
'Cos Nick is a wanker!
Nick is the captain of the ship,
Of our ship!"

Zulu Warrior
Get it down you Zulu Warrior,
get it down you Zulu…
CHIEF, CHIEF, CHIEF!

Yellow Submarine
In the town were I was born,
Lived a man called Nick Casey,
And he sailed along the sea,
In his yellow submarine…
Nick Casey is a homosexual*,
A homosexual! (*Louder*)
A homosexual! (*Louder*)

*If you don't feel calling someone a homosexual as an insult is entirely
PC you can insert 'total fucking **cunt**' here, or any insult you like.

Our Mate in Eight
Ohhh… we like to drink with Nicky (you always add a 'Y' to the name)
'Cos Nicky is our mate
And when we drink with Nicky he gets it down in eight!
Eight,
Seven,
Six,
Five,
Four,
Three,
Two,
One,
Wa-hay! (this comes when the drink is finished, so it could be after any
number).

All of these songs are fairly short, the idea being that the drinker should finish his or her drink before the song is finished. If they don't manage to do it, then the embarrassment created by the deadly silence will increase the pressure to finish. If a group reaches the end of a song they will sometimes point and shout, "Who are ya? Who are ya?" (in the style of football fans). The implication is, "You're not one of us!")

The psychology of peer pressure will force even the strongest-willed into drinking, for no one likes to feel left out. Furthermore, overcoming your fear of a fine earns you esteem within the group. If someone absolutely refuses a fine they are said to be a **splinter**.

Player 6 is encouraged to drink by all the other players

Pick up on
If you pick up on something you start to understand it. The expression describes the process in your head whereby you use little clues to solve a bigger puzzle. When learning a drinking game, you often understand little bits before the logic of the whole game dawns upon you.

Pinky finger, Pinkies
Your pinky is usually the smallest finger on your hand, though I have seen some people with freakish looking hands so it's probably safer to say it's the furthest finger from the thumb. Maybe it's called pinky

because its pinker than the rest, but I've never noticed any colour difference in my pinky fingers!

Pint see **Dirty pint (D)**

Piss
1. To piss yourself is to laugh hysterically. The expression refers to the problem of involuntary urination that can occur when laughing uncontrollably.

2. Piss is also a crude way to say drink.

Pissed
Another name for being drunk. Probably the term refers to the increased frequency of bathroom visitation during drinking, is also used because, in extreme cases, very drunk people actually urinate themselves.

Other words and phrases for being intoxicated with alcohol are: **cunted**, bladdered, on a bender (this describes the time **out**[2] as well as getting drunk), skulled, mashed up, **fucked**[2], twatted, shit-faced, pickled, smashed, plastered, **lashed**, battered, tanked up, drunk, blotto, **wrecked**, wankered, mangled, bollocksed… and many, many more.

Pissed off
To be annoyed, angry or upset with a thing, another person or oneself.

No pointing
Some people claim there is such a thing as **International Drinking Rules (I)**. There is no actual international body for the creation of drinking rule legislation, but if such a body did exist it could be argued that one of their first rules should be 'no pointing'. 'No pointing' is simple but effective. You don't realise how much you point until the privilege is taken from you. If anyone points when 'no pointing' rules have been instigated they are punished. Furthermore, if the pointing transgression takes place in a game where it is disadvantageous to have the **go** then the go will pass to them as an extra forfeit after the fine has been taken.

A poisoned chalice
Something that initially appears to be rewarding but actually harms the person who receives it.

Poker

Poker is a card game, which has become very popular in recent times. Players gamble on the superior value of card combinations called hands. They place their bets (which usually, though not always, have a monetary value) in an established sequence, into a central **pot**. The winner is the player who holds the hand with the highest value according to a set hierarchy, or the last player remains in the round after all others have folded (i.e. gone **out**[1]).

Polish

To polish something off is to finish it. This comes from the sense of adding the polish, always the last job when you clean something.

e.g. "Polish off that drink, Kelly."

Pot

A term used to describe a communal vessel to which everyone contributes. A pot is requisite in 'Arrogance' (p26) and 'The Challenge' (p16). The idea of the pot comes from the pot in **Poker**, the total sum of money wagered in a round, usually placed in the centre of the table.

A communal vessel or pot

The power

If you've got the power, it's your turn or **go**. You are the one everyone looks to as you perform an action or specific **call**[1].

Pre-lash

This saying is rather silly as pre-lash is **lash**. It implies that it is a period of drinking before the *real* drinking (i.e. the lash) begins. In reality it is the pre-lash that gets you drunk. It's a period of drinking before you head **out**[2] for the night. Pre-lash is undertaken with a group of friends usually to get everyone in the **festive** mood, or even **pissed**, depending on the level of the lash being orchestrated.

Pre-lash is university inspired as no one has enough money to get drunk in the club or bar they intend to visit, so they lash before they get there in order to turn up drunk. The rather bizarre logic behind this is that you will spend less money once you there. Unfortunately, once drunk, your self-restraint dissolves and this plan will often fail.

Pull, Pulling (also see **Pulling Rank (R)**)

The practice of attracting the opposite sex (or same sex depending on how you're inclined) in order to dance, kiss and perhaps if you're lucky, have sexual relations. A pull is usually not a long-term sort of relationship, as you are together with that person for only one night, (though you could regularly pull the same person). Being **out**[2] on the pull is to go looking for these types of relations on a night out.

e.g. "We're out on the pull tonight... WAHAAAYYYYY!" or "I've pulled him before."

Pull it back

To pull something back is to win despite adversity. One of the greatest examples of this is Liverpool's 2005 victory in the European Cup.

The put in

1. An imaginary zone where bets or amounts are held (in a figurative sense) until guesses have been made.

2. The time or place at which a bet is revealed.

3. An offering.

Q

A quick game's a good game

This expression is often used in drinking games in order to keep the play fast. Certain drinking games, particularly **circle go games (C)** require fast play to ensure that players do not have too much time to calculate their next move or moves. As the **Administrator** it is your job to judge and implement the appropriate speed for the game you are playing.

R

Racking up

If fines or scores are racking up, the total is getting ever higher. An expression based on old-fashioned scorecards which were literally hung on a rack.

e.g. "Oh my god, the fines are racking up for you Phil!"

Rainbow yawn

An Australian expression describing being sick. See also **bunder**[1] and **chunder**.

Pull rank, Pulling rank

This saying has come from the military, where senior-ranking officers may use their position to secure benefits and privileges.

e.g. Lieutenant Teddington: "What happened, Scotty?"
Lieutenant Scott: "I was watching T.V. in the mess but the Major came in with the civvies (civvies is short for civilians i.e. non-military) he's showing round and pulled rank, so I had to give up my seat."

In the civilian world it is less clear who your social superiors are. Basically they are anyone who you are willing to have tell you what to do, e.g. a girlfriend or boyfriend, your parents, someone who you're frightened of, someone you envy or someone who is older than you. Most of the time you will be unaware that you view them in this way, but if they asked you for something then 90% of the time you would give them what they wanted. Giving your boss or your parents, what they want is usually passed off as a social grace, but there is more psychology behind it than you might expect.

Rattle off
Say something quickly, like a machine gun discharging bullets, tap-tap-tap-tap-tap-tap!

Repeat offender
A player who commits a transgression against the rules of a game and then makes the same mistake again. They are punished twice and look particularly foolish for not learning from their first mistake.

Roll-off
A dice competition to see who can roll the highest score. If two people have joint-highest scores then they have another roll-off between themselves. Roll-offs are usually used to find who goes first in a specific game.

Roll-up, Roll-ups
Slang term for a hand-made cigarette.

Roman numerals
A system of counting using symbols that equate to specific numerical values (see table below). The system originated in ancient Rome and then was slightly modified in the Middle Ages to give the system we know today.

Symbol	Value
I	1 (one)
V	5 (five)
X	10 (ten)
L	50 (fifty)
C	100 (one hundred)
D	500 (five hundred)
M	1,000 (one thousand)

Numbers not assigned a specific symbol below can be created by combining symbols, e.g. VIII = 8 and IV = 4.

Rounds

1. Rounds of drinks. In the rounds system, people buy drinks for the group. This allows drinks to be bought communally without having to establish a **kitty**.

Let's say, for example's sake, there are four people drinking and every drink costs £2. Instead of each person finding £2 in change whenever they want a drink, the drinkers enter into a sort of unnegotiated pact. At the core of this pact is the premise that every drinker will drink at least four drinks. One person uses his or her money to buy drinks for the whole group. When these have been drunk the next person buys, and so on until everyone in the group has bought a round. At this point everything is equal and no one has had to search for change or talk about money.

The system I've described above needs no explanation to regular pub or bar drinkers. However, there are problems with the rounds system:
- some people don't understand the concept and bring up debts they are owed from a time before the round began
- some people choose drinks that are more expensive than the drinks others in the group are having and the price of drinking rises for all
- sometimes, if you **get in (G²)** an early round, paying the maximum amount, the round may not be returned and you can feel cheated.

My advice is that unless you are **out²** with very like-minded people, or don't mind getting ripped off, you shouldn't enter into rounds in Britain because no one seems to honour them. On the Continent, in general, people are better at sharing, probably because they are used to receiving bills for drinks rather than paying up front. When I was in Holland I found a group in a bar can run a tab on drinks and settle up at the end… can you imagine that happening in a city centre near you? We'd all **do a runner (R)**!

2. Rounds of play. A round is a unitary amount by which games can be measured. When everyone in a game has had a turn, or at least the chance of a turn, the round has finished. A round usually finishes at a point of equilibrium i.e. when everyone playing has had one turn or **go**. However, a round can also be completed when the game breaks down

after a mistake. When the game restarts after the mistake, this is said to be a new round.

Some games can conclude after one round but most games take more than one round to find a winner or loser. In some games, e.g. 'Ring of Fire' (p185) you play one round of one game and then another round of another game.

Ruffneck
In patois (a Jamaican-English blended language) this means rough neck i.e. a tough guy or hard thing.

You might hear someone from **St. Pauls (S)** in Bristol say "U no dat ruffneck ting?" in other words, "Do you know about being tough?" 'Da ruffneck ting' literally means being a gangster or a wide boy.

To do a runner
To do a runner is to run off without paying or to escape from a difficult situation.

e.g. "He's done a runner!", the prison guard exclaimed, as the prisoner jumped over the wall.

Russian roulette
A potentially lethal game in which a bullet is placed in one or more of the chambers of a revolver. The cylinder is spun and quickly closed so that the location of the round or rounds is unknown. Each player in turn then points the revolver at their own head and pulls the trigger, risking death from a gunshot wound. Not the brightest of ideas but I'm sure it would make you feel alive if you heard the 'click'! There is a famous Russian roulette scene in the film *The Deer Hunter* (1978).

S
A good Samaritan
A person who thinks of others before him or herself. The term comes from the Bible, where a Samaritan helps a man who has been beaten up while all others walk pass. I use Samaritan in the sense of the antithesis to a **cunt** in 'Stop the Bus!' (p163).

Savage (also see **lash** for savage lash)
If something is savage it is difficult and **hardcore**.

e.g. "That ski run was savage!"

In terms of drinking, savage describes a extreme drinking **session**. Savage steps outside normal bounds and is extreme in the way it is undertaken and the results.

Off the scent
To lose what you are tracking, your way or your direction. The expression originates from the practice of using dogs such as bloodhounds and beagles to track using scent. If you put someone off the scent by your actions in a game you deceive them into taking a wrong turn.

Scout sign, Scout's sign
The Scouts, famed for their pseudo-military rituals, have a sign that is used when they are sworn in and is in constant use after the ceremony. People sometimes make the sign when they sarcastically say, "Scouts honour."

To perform this salute your index finger, middle finger and ring finger are held up while the **pinky finger (P)** is held down with the thumb. The arm is outstretched at shoulder height and the elbow bent upwards at 90° degrees. The palm of the hand faces outwards.

I mention the boy scout sign because both hands should be held in this way when performing the third stage of 'I'm Colonel Puff' (p141).

**Scout sign — the same as Colonel Puff (pXX)
when you tap three times**

Screw, Screws, Screwed

1. If you are screwed or someone screws you, you have been placed in a disadvantageous position. Usually if you say you've been screwed you're implying that the person doing the screwing has created the situation on purpose, for malicious reasons.

e.g. "The taxman has screwed me again!"

Or after Ben phones in 'sick' for work, Dan is left on his own on a really busy shift. Dan says, "Ben has really screwed me this time!"

If you find yourself in a compromised situation you may exclaim, "I'm fucking screwed!" This has the same meaning as **fucked**[1].

2. To screw is to have sexual intercourse on a casual basis.

e.g. "We screw from time to time."
(Though I'd say you'd more likely use 'fuck' in this context.)

See off

Finish your drink. This is often expressed as a demand or order, in which case it literally translates as 'ensure your drink is finished'.

Even though the expression suggests that the drinker completes the task of their own free will, the reality is that the person who told them to see it off will watch them finish their drink.

If you have to see off your drink during a game it usually means that you have transgressed. You may also be **called**[3] to see off your drink when you are just about to leave for a night **out**[2]. In the latter situation the order is likely to be preceded by the call "**Everything wet must go (E)!**"

Session, Sessions

A period of time in which drinking takes place is often called a session. The expression translates drinking into sporting terms, implying a training session. Usually if you were having a relaxed drink this would not be regarded as a session. It is usually only when **lash** is present that the time spent drinking is called a session.

e.g. "Let's **get**[4] on a big session tonight!" or "That was one **hell of a (H)** session last night!"

A shoeing

A shoeing is slang for when someone gets beaten up. It is descriptive of the beating you receive if you fall to the floor in a street fight, i.e. you get kicked by shoes!

However, a shoeing as far as *The Lash* is concerned is when someone offers a shoe as a vessel to drink from. A fine (usually some considerable amount) is poured into the shoe and the guilty party drinks the punishment from the shoe. A tip on technique: drink from the heel and not the side.

A nice little punishment!

Short, Shorts

A measure of **spirits** in a small shot glass. Shorts usually come in either a single (25ml) or a double (50ml) measure.

Shotgun, Shot-gunning, Shot-gunned (also see **bagsy**)

To shotgun something is to make claims on it. The shotgun procedure is used to lay claim to a seat in the front of the car, or anything else you want. Historically speaking, shotgun was the position next to the driver on a stagecoach, where the guard sat with a gun to ward-off highwaymen.

If there are more than three people getting into the car and no one has a status claim (if you're travelling with both your parents, it's unlikely that you'll get to ride in the front because your parents **pull rank (R)** over you) then shotgun calling helps avoid any dispute over who gets to ride in the front. The first person to say 'shotgun' gets to sit next to the driver. You can only call 'shotgun' when you can actually see the vehicle in question.

Shot-gunning has come along way from it roots in motor vehicle seat allocation and now basically anything can be shot-gunned so long as you make clear what you are shotgunning and you are able to see it.

e.g. "Shotgun the last cake!", "Shotgun that computer!" or "Shotgun the T.V. remote!"

You can also 'shotgun not' something. This is where you make a claim in order to get out of doing something undesirable. The last person to say "shotgun not" will have to perform the task.

A final word on shotgunning: I have one extra rule, which is that you can't shotgun members of the opposite sex (or the same sex, depending on how you're inclined) for all is fair in love and war.

Shout

To shout someone something, is to offer to pay for it.

e.g. "I'll **get**[2] the drinks in. It's my shout."

This is different from a **round**[1] because in a round the payment is ultimately shared. A shout is just a kind gesture.

Skittles

An old European target sport, which is a variety of bowling. The game is most common in pubs in the counties of south west England.

A slab

An Australian slang term for twenty-four **beers**. The term describes the way the beers are packaged in a rectangular slab.

A slab — 24 beers!

You snooze, you lose
A good saying to use when you are first to do something which other people wish they had done.

e.g. Matt takes the last **beer** from the fridge and exclaims to the other lads who look on enviously, "Sorry, boys. You snooze, you lose!"

This phrase is a clear statement that if you are not **on the ball (B)** you will lose out because of your inertia.

Soft, Softer
The opposite to hard, as in tough. The expression has a sexual connotation of not being able to get a hard-on, i.e. erection. If someone is being soft they are displaying a lack of fortitude or virility, i.e. they are feeble, weak or effeminate. Usually men will tease other men soft if they are not displaying perceived masculine characteristics.

e.g. Nick looks wide-eyed at the **dirty pint (D)** in front of him.
Luke says, "Don't be soft, **man up (M)**!

If you were to go soft as the **Administrator** you would be lenient with the rules and fine amounts. *The Lash's* motto is: "Go hard or go home!" However, every drinking **session** is different, so sometimes you may need to be a little softer.

S.O.P.
Standard Operating Procedure is a **T.L.A**.

Sopwith Camel
The plane preferred by **Biggles**. The Camel was a British, First World War, single-seat fighter aircraft, famous for its manoeuvrability.

Drink spiked
Not a laughing matter. This is when someone puts a drug into your drink in a bar, pub or club. The drug makes you either forget everything that happens or makes you unable to master your actions. The very fact that the effects of drink spiking mirror those of extreme drunkenness often leaves the victim open to the advances of an assailant. Often the assailant uses the drug to give them the opportunity to sexually assault or rape their victim. Usually, but not always, young women are the victims.

There has certainly been more media coverage of 'date rape' incidents in recent years and I have heard about people who have collapsed for no apparent reason after one or two drinks at university. Something to watch out for, especially if you're female.

Spirits
Spirits are distilled beverages, low in sugars and containing at least 35% alcohol by volume. The best-known spirits are gin, rum, vodka and whisky. Spirits will turn any drinking **session** very **savage** indeed!

Splinter
Someone who does not fit in with group dynamics. They might call themselves an individual, but you can be an individual within a group, so it is really someone who doesn't want to 'play by the rules'. Splinters either ostracize themselves from the group or are rejected by the group. I particularly dislike splinters as they often spoil things for everyone else playing a game. A splinter is often a selfish or anti-social person.

The term splinter is based on the idea that they have sheared off from the main body, i.e. the group, which in this case is figuratively represented by an unblemished piece of wood. To extend this metaphor, a splinter disrupts the unity and strength of the wood (i.e. the group) and is an unwelcome and potentially harmful defect.

A splinter ruins the game for all!

Spot on
This has been a Carling™ tagline in its time. It means to get something exactly right. See also **on the nose (N)**.

Stakes

The amount bet, invested or ventured on a specific outcome. The higher the stake the more there is to win but also the more there is to lose.

Starbucks™

The trading name for a multinational coffee house chain.

In a state

To be in a state is to be so drunk that your personal appearance is affected (also see **wrecked**). You might be so **pissed** that you look awful; hair like you've been dragged through a bush, blood all over you from where you fell over and perhaps a lazy eye from not being able to focus. If you're acting and looking something like this because of drink, then you're in a state!

Stein, steiner

Large **beer** glass that can contain up to a litre of liquid. Most frequently found in European countries especially Germanic nations. You can improvise with a **beer** jug or a large **tankard** at your local.

Step in

If you step in you take charge of a situation. When stepping in as the **Administrator** of a game, you take charge and dispense justice and make decisions where necessary.

Step up

I'm not completely sure about this, but it may come from the American baseball term 'step up to the plate'. The plate is an area on the ground over which the bat is swung and is where the batter will receive balls thrown by the pitcher. The saying has come to mean to galvanise yourself in the face of adversity. If you 'step up' you come forward and take action. It can also mean to raise your game, i.e. put in a better performance than usual in order to succeed. See also **man up (M)**.

e.g. "Tiger Woods stepped up at The Masters."
"Don't be a coward, STEP UP!"
"If you're going to win, you need to step up."

Stiefel
A boot-shaped drinking vessel often found on the Continent, particularly in Germanic nations.

Stitch, Stiched, Stitch up, Stich them up
When you deliberately play a game in such a way that fines fall on a person or group of people you want to be punished. This is always done in the spirit of fun and mostly (though not exclusively) conducted within the rules of the game.

A good example of a stitch is the following situation in '21' (p82):

The **go** comes to you on '17' and you say "18, 19, 20" so that the person two places further on will have to **chin** his or her pint. You have 'stitched' them, as in theory you could reversed it with "18, 19." Instead you chose to make them drink. Thus you stitched him or her up.

If you are stitched up or stitched you have usually been tricked or fooled into a disadvantageous position. In terms of drinking games you might have been left by another player with no other option than to incur a fine. I suppose the saying come from the fact that your options have been restricted, i.e. sewn up or stitched up.

St. Pauls
An area of Bristol known for its Afro-Caribbean community. Once a year it holds the St. Pauls Carnival. Often people who don't know the city will hold up St. Pauls as an example of an area of the city that is riddled with crime. I suppose I'm only reinforcing the idea by linking the term **ruffneck** to the area.

Straights
A colloquialism for a machine-produced cigarette, which usually comes in a carton or pack.

Strawpedo
Put a straw in a bottle of **beer** or alcopop and then bend the top section of the straw over the lip. Then place your hand round the neck of the bottle insuring that you are not obstructing the straw. Tip the bottle upside down and drink the liquid – don't just pour, suck. You'll be surprised at the results. The straw forces the beer down your throat with

a vacuum-type action. You'll be able to impress your friends with the speed at which you can **see off (S)** a bottle. I've seen whole bottles of wine, i.e. 750ml, strawpedoed but perhaps you should build up to this by practising with smaller bottles.

A quick way to see off any amount of drink in a bottle — just add a straw!

Stubby
These are the small bottled **beers** of robust stature with a short neck.

T

Tankard
A cylindrical drinking vessel with a big handle, usually seen in the hands of a local at the bar. It often has a glass or clear bottom, which is a tradition stretching back to the days of enforced recruitment to the armed forces by press gangs. Members of a press gang used to go into pubs and taverns and drop a 'King's shilling' into customers' drinks. If anyone finished a drink with the coin in this was seen as a sign that they accepted service. In response, people created glass-bottomed drinking vessels so they could check for the King's shilling before drinking – hence the saying 'bottoms up'.

T.L.A.
Three Letter Abbreviation. Every circle, clique, industry and lifestyle has these. The greatest example is the Military.

I hate it when people talk in T.L.A. as it excludes others from the conversation. It's not big and it's not clever to talk in T.L.A's if no-one knows what you're on about. Often if people aren't that intelligent they use T.L.A.'s to mask their ignorance and pretend they have some sort of information superiority over others.

Next time someone uses a T.L.A. on you, just say "I'm **N.F.I.** in T.L.A's!".

Top Gun
A 1986 film staring Tom Cruise. The film follows a young Naval aviator, Lt Pete 'Maverick' Mitchell as he struggles to be the best of the best at Miramar, an elite pilot training school.

The sound you create making a jet in the 'Captain Bigglesworth' variation of 'Bunnies' (p124) should sound something like the opening scene of *Top Gun* as the **F-14 Tomcat** flies off the end of the aircraft carrier.

Top row
Where the **spirits** are kept on a bar. Anything from the top row is likely to be quite nasty and strong. Usually in the game 'Four Aces' (p19) the person buying the drink adds something from the top row. A visit to the top row is a requisist for a good **dirty pint (D)**.

Tour, On tour, Touring party
A touring party is a group of people travelling around a specific area with a specific aim in mind. You can go on a cultural tour to take in all the major sights of a specific country.

However, the type of tour most associated with drinking is the sports tour (which may or may not be serious). There are also the institutions known as: 'girls on tour' or 'lads on tour'. These sorts of tours are a British phenomenon and consist of drinking and **debauchery**. They used to mainly take place in the summer in the Mediterranean, but thanks to cheap flights they are spreading all over the world throughout the year. God bless Blighty for it's major cultural export – drunken violence!

On tour there is a carnival atmosphere where drinking and sex are usually the most favoured activities. A serious drinking tour has many quirks and traditions, e.g. the **Gopher**.

Trestle table

The sort of table that you see at Jubilee celebrations and in pictures of the street parties that took place at the end of the Second World War. The tables are rectangular, usually (though not always) wooden and have legs that fold away underneath (and are not usually all that stable).

This is the perfect type of table for 'Beer Pong' (p147) due to its height from the floor and length from end to end.

Triple a triple

In many drinking games the **go** skips one player when a word is said three times or an action is done three times. You are not usually allowed to do this more than twice in a row. If anyone does triple a triple, you should say "You can't triple a triple!" and fine the player who did the tripling.

Trough, Troughing

This is a feeling of mental and physical tiredness, which can be tinged by depression but, more specifically, a feeling that everything is too much, i.e. the world is a frightening place when you sober up. The first scene of *Withnail and I* **(W)** depicts a trough in the Camden Café.

A trough must not be confused with a hangover. A hangover is generally a feeling of sickness and comes with symptoms that are more physical than a feeling or attitude.

A trough is that feeling you get when you eat too much Christmas turkey. It is the drinker's version of a **comedown**. I also use trough in the sense of having a bad day, e.g. "I'm in a bit of a trough today". It's a way of describing an emotional state without being as melodramatic as saying, "I'm a bit depressed."

Trough comes from the science term for the low point on a wave or graph.

Tune

A really great song or aural experience. This is usually marked by a 'T' sign made with either the fingers or two whole hands. See photo opposite.

e.g. "That was a tune!"

Made with either an arm (like this) or fingers

Twiglets™
The brand name for a savoury snack consisting of nobbly bread sticks covered in a Marmite™ type brown substance. The scourge of children's parties – and later in life, **dirty pints (D)**!

U
U.D.I.
An Unidentified Drinking Injury. A **T.L.A**. After a **heavy** night out[2] it is not unusual to wake up with a split head or massively sore leg and not know where it has come from. These are U.D.I.s. Your drink-addled brain is generally unable to make sense of the way injuries and blemishes have magically materialised on your body!

Underhand, Underhanded
Underhand behaviour is dishonest, and may involve deception and disguise. I guess the saying comes from passing things without showing them, as you would a bribe or such-like.

Unmentionable words
Certain words in drinking games cannot be mentioned for fear of punishment. The two best examples are 'twenty-one' in '21' (p82), which is usually referred to as 'twenty plus one' and 'drink' which is often known as 'the D-word' under **International Drinking Rules (I)**. It is also prohibited in 'Master of the Three' (p48).

Urban
This is a term used to describe hip-hop culture or subsets of black culture. For me urban is less about race and more about a style of living that embraces the city. Urban refers to the fact that there is more happening in cities compared to suburbs or rural areas.

A person who can be described as 'urban' is often young, connected and interested in culture and music. I believe urban incorporates all types of dance music (drum and bass, jungle etc.) not just R&B and hip-hop.

Urban also incorporates sports such as freerunning (see **parcour**) and skating.

V
Varsity
Varsity is a colloquial term for university. Varsity sports matches usually take place between rival universities like Oxford and Cambridge, like the varsity boat race is an annual competition in rowing between Oxford and Cambridge on the Thames. The highest standard of Rugby Union varsity is usually (though not always) a match between Bath and Loughborough as both universities champion themselves as the premier sports establishments in England.

Veteran, Veterans
A military term used in drinking game terminology to describe someone with prior playing experience as well as theoretical knowledge of the game.

W

Wasted

To be wasted is to be totally **pissed**, i.e. drunk. So drunk that you literally can't control yourself. Wasted also means to be killed but I am not using the word in this sense in *The Lash*. You may also want to reference **casualty**, **veteran** and **man down (M)** to learn how drinking terminology and war fighting terminology often overlap.

The West Country

The south west of England. Known for its farmer-like accent, cider and love for Rugby Union.

Whip round

This is when a person from the group asks everyone to contribute money to a communal cause, usually drink-related. This may be contributing to a **kitty** or to a **dirty pint (D)** for a member of the group.

Withnail and I

Withnail and I is a cult British film from 1986. It was Richard E. Grant's first film role. The film is about the misadventures of two unemployed actors in 1969.

There is a drinking game in which you try and drink everything that the characters drink in *Withnail and I*. This can include lighter fluid, often depending on how **savage** you want the **session** to become!

Wreck, Wrecked

Wrecked literally means drunk (see **pissed**). It is more descriptive than simple labels, for to be wrecked is to be so intoxicated that you are slurring your words and moving with poor co-ordination as you are most likely **in a state (S)**. If you're wrecked you've lost all self-respect, your clothes are probably torn from that detour between pubs and you've been sick on yourself.

Y

Yard glass

A British drinking vessel, which contains 2.5 pints and is characterised by its bulbous end. When you drink from a proper yard you need to turn it slowly as you drink because otherwise the liquid will approach your mouth in waves.

Yokel

This is a local, usually a farmer or country person that has lived in the same area for a long time. A yoke is a farming term for the piece of equipment that used to go over a beast of burden like an ox or horse to displace the weight of the plough over the animals' shoulders. So the word yokel combines the words 'yoke' and 'local'.

Z

Zamboney

If a drink is spilt someone might call "ZAMBONEY!" This is the cue for the person who spilt their drink to suck the drink off whatever surface they spilt it onto. The zamboney **call**[1] pays lip service (ha! do you like what I've done there?) to the idea that drink is a precious commodity and should not be wasted.

Obviously, zamboney calls are usually rejected unless you are on a really ruthless **session**!

Don't ask me why it's called zamboney. It just is. Another etymological mystery like **buffalo**.

Zoom a zoomer

In general terms this means you can't give the **go** back to the person who sent the go to you. The term comes from the game 'Zoom, Schwartz, Pafigliano' (p71).

Printed in the United Kingdom
by Lightning Source UK Ltd.
135030UK00001B/286-288/P